WELCOMING BLUE-COLLAR SCHOLARS INTO THE IVORY TOWER

Developing Class-Conscious Strategies for Student Success

Krista M. Soria

D1205606

Contents

Foreword v
Tracy L. Skipper, Series Editor

Chapter 1
Introduction 1

Chapter 2
Theoretical Perspectives on Social Class in Higher Education 11

Chapter 3
**Access to Higher Education: Examining the Roots of Disparities
in Attendance and Attainment** 19

Chapter 4
Class in the Class(ed)room 29

Chapter 5
Social Class and Integration on Campus 43

Chapter 6
**Strategies for Campuswide Reform to Support Working-Class
Students in Transition** 53

References 69

Index 87

About the Author 91

Foreword

Tracy L. Skipper
Series Editor

Much of the work of the National Resource Center for The First-Year Experience and Students in Transition has focused on examining the structures that support student learning, development, and success—whether they be first-year seminars, learning communities, orientation programs, senior capstones, residential learning initiatives, service-learning experiences, or common reading programs. A second focal point of our work has been understanding the nature of student transitions within higher education, including the transition into college, the sophomore year, transfer between institutions, the senior year, and the transition into graduate study and the workplace. In addition, we have explored the unique populations of students entering postsecondary education and how we might better support their access, learning, and success. To that end, we have published on the needs of students with learning disabilities, student athletes, and students of color.

Nearly a decade after publishing *Transforming the First Year of College for Students of Color* (Rendón, García, & Person, 2004), we turned our attention once again to the needs and experiences of specific student populations, launching a call for a new books series on this topic. In her conclusion to that earlier monograph, Rendón (2004) argued that providing a transformational experience for underrepresented students in the first college year was about more than putting initiatives in place and creating learning environments that would support academic success and retention. Rather, she argued, transformation must "also include a social justice agenda that challenges existing structures and those they privilege, favoring democratic structural changes where power and privilege are shared among different constituencies" (p. 177). In launching the call for this new book series, Rendón's charge was before us, as was the work of more recent higher education scholars.

For example, Estela Bensimon (Harris & Bensimon, 2007; Witham & Bensimon, 2012) has noted that, historically, differential outcomes for racial or ethnic minority students have been attributed to the students' background or experiences rather than institutional values, policies, or practices that might adversely affect learning or success. This same logic might extend to any number of student populations who do not fit the increasingly narrow definition of the typical U.S. college student—that is, students with physical, learning, or intellectual disabilities; GLBTQ students; military veterans; adult learners; international students; and students from low socioeconomic backgrounds, among others. In other words, institutions tend to adopt a problem-solving posture when they encounter students who are atypical, creating new programs or policies to remediate perceived deficits within the identified student population. While such efforts frequently lead to improved learning and increased retention and graduation rates in the target population, they leave the structure of higher education essentially unchanged—meaning that each new student group fights the battle for access and success anew and institutions create a host of boutique programs that replicate services and initiatives found elsewhere on the campus. Problem-solving approaches may also send the subtle, but often unmistakable, message that the student must be fixed in order to fit into the campus community, succeed within a particular program of study, or earn a degree. Students may reject this message (and higher education along with it), or they may experience the kind of doubt that will lead to their failure. Thus, the problem-solving approach may undermine the very success it seeks to ensure.

In exploring the learning and transition experiences of diverse student populations in U.S. higher education, we hoped to move beyond a deficit model. As such, we invited proposals that critically examined some of the fundamental assumptions underlying student success initiatives with an eye toward reshaping campus cultures, policies, and practices to support students from underrepresented or nontraditional populations. We hoped to produce resources about student experiences and needs that took a problem-questioning rather than problem-solving approach. The problem-questioning view shifts the focus of study from the student group in isolation to the student group within the larger social, cultural, and institutional contexts of U.S. postsecondary education. Rather than asking what types of skills, knowledge, and dispositions the student needs to succeed, it asks what characteristics of this environment facilitate (or hinder) learning, success, and development. Instead of boutique programs that serve the needs of specific groups, problem-questioning approaches engender broader cultural transformation that support all students to reach their educational goals. Finally, by focusing on the larger context instead of individual students or groups of students, problem-questioning approaches recognize the inherent value of everyone entering the educational environment.

This first book in our series on special student populations in U.S. higher education focuses on students from working-class backgrounds. In a recent op-ed in *The Chronicle of Higher Education*, Wolin (2012) lamented the faded glory of American higher education, noting, "During [the 1960s and 1970s], colleges functioned as crucial mechanisms of democratization and social inclusion. Today they are repositioning themselves as bastions of class privilege and social exclusion" (para. 5). Indeed, even as President Barack Obama and others have called for increased access to higher education, growing income inequality has made this more difficult not only for low-income students but for their middle-class counterparts as well. To the students from low-income and working-class backgrounds, or whose families have fallen out of the middle class, who somehow manage to arrive on our campuses, higher education—especially within selective institutions—may seem increasingly foreign.

Indeed, as law professor and civil rights theorist Lani Grunier (2015) recently observed, pervasive beliefs in meritocracy may lead colleges and universities—particularly those highly invested in the rankings race—to shift their missions from one of talent development to confirming the achievement of those they admit. In other words, "colleges would perform little more than sorting functions, cherry-picking students who have come up the escalator of excellence and arrived at their doorsteps presumably prepackaged and pre-equipped with everything they need for success" (para. 8). To the extent that students from working-class backgrounds arrive on campus without at least some of the requisite packaging, they may find higher education challenging at best and inhospitable at worst.

In their exhaustive study of access to higher education among low-income students, Carnevale and Strohl (2010) highlight a two-prong concern: Low-income and working-class students have lower rates of participation in postsecondary education than middle- and upper-income students, but they are also likely to be concentrated in less-selective institutions where graduation rates are lower and career opportunities are fewer. As a result of this vertical stratification of higher education, the rich (both in terms of real wealth and in terms of educational opportunity or advantage) get richer. Carnevale and Strohl suggest that we need to create greater parity among institutions so that outcomes (e.g., degree attainment, job placement, career advancement opportunities, earning capacity) are equalized across the system. We also need to get larger numbers of low-income students into more selective and better-resourced institutions where they have greater likelihood of achieving their personal and educational goals. The structural issues surrounding the vertical stratification of U.S. higher education are beyond the scope of this volume. Instead, Krista Soria focuses on the latter concern—how do we increase participation among low-income and working-class students and how do we create environments that will retain them and help them succeed?

The current volume opens by describing who working-class college students are and the relationship between the myth of meritocracy and social mobility in contemporary U.S. culture. Using the theory of social reproduction as a lens, Soria explores access to and experiences in the academic and social spaces of the campus. The chapters on classroom and social environments include recommendations for transforming those spaces to better support students from working-class backgrounds. Finally, the book concludes with a chapter on strategies for campuswide reform.

This series is designed to continue the conversation we began more than a decade ago with the publication of *Transforming the First Year of College for Students of Color*. We hope that readers find both theoretical grounding and practical strategies for beginning the process of transformation on their own campuses. As always, we welcome your feedback on this volume and your suggestions for future volumes in this series.

References

Carnevale, A. P., & Strohl, J. (2010). How increasing college access is increasing inequality, and what to do about it. In R. D. Kahlenberg (Ed.), *Rewarding strivers: Helping low-income students succeed in college* (pp. 71-187). Washington, DC: The Century Foundation Press.

Grunier, L. (2015, January 5). The tyranny of meritocracy. *The Chronicle of Higher Education*. Retrieved from http://chronicle.com.

Harris, F., III, & Bensimon, E. M. (2007). The Equity Scorecard: A collaborative approach to assess and respond to racial/ethnic disparities in student outcomes. *New Directions for Student Service, 120,* 77-84. doi: 10.1002/ss.259.

Rendón, L. I. (2004). Transforming the first-year experience for students of color: Where do we begin? In L. I. Rendón, M. García, & D. Person (Eds.). *Transforming the first year of college for students of color* (Monograph No. 38, pp. 177-184). Columbia, SC: University of South Carolina, National Resource Center for The First-Year Experience & Students in Transition.

Rendón, L. I., García, M., & Person, D. (Eds.). (2004). *Transforming the first year of college for students of color* (Monograph No. 38). Columbia, SC: University of South Carolina, National Resource Center for The First-Year Experience & Students in Transition.

Witham, K. A., & Bensimon, E. M. (2012). Creating a culture of inquiry around equity and student success. In S. D. Museus & U. M. Jayakumar (Eds.), *Creating campus cultures: Fostering success among racially diverse student populations* (pp. 46-67). New York, NY: Routledge.

Wolin, R. (2012, July 2). Fading glory days. *The Chronicle of Higher Education*. Retrieved from http://chronicle.com.

Chapter 1
INTRODUCTION

The dominant, driving narrative framing U.S. society is the continual pursuit of upward social mobility; yet, for college students from working-class backgrounds, the pathways to higher education and economic mobility are fraught with obstacles. The social system of higher education embodies middle- and upper-class cultural values, norms, and perspectives, and it privileges those who occupy prestigious social locations (Banks, 2009; Green, 2003; Hurst, 2010, 2012; Pearce, Down, & Moore, 2008; Reay, David, & Ball, 2001; Stuber, 2011). As a consequence, college students from working-class backgrounds have significantly more difficult transitions to the unfamiliar territory of higher education than their middle- and upper-class peers. These are, in part, cultural transitions—working-class students often struggle with renegotiating aspects of their identities as they find themselves balancing the families and communities of their upbringing and the middle-class culture of higher education. According to Jensen (2012), these class-based cultural barriers are "at least as effective in shutting out working-class people as the significant economic barriers to college education" (p. 156).

The consequences of these tenuous transitions to higher education have long-term negative ramifications for working-class students' educational pathways and career opportunities. It is nearly axiomatic that earning a college degree will enhance one's economic prosperity and stability (Callan, 2011; Carnevale & Desrochers, 2003; Immerwahr, Johnson, Ott, & Rochkind, 2010); however, several decades' worth of research has substantiated that students from working-class backgrounds are significantly less likely to enter four-year higher education institutions, persist, and graduate with baccalaureate degrees than their peers from middle- and upper-class backgrounds. Summarizing the concerns underlying these disparities, Oldfield (2012) noted succinctly, "those who can stand to most benefit from college are least likely to attend" (p. 9). In fact, Hurst (2012) estimated only 3% of the working class would earn a college degree in their lifetimes.

Yet, colleges and universities have systematically neglected social class as an important element of diversity on campus and have not considered the unique needs and experiences of students from working-class backgrounds in recruitment or after enrollment. If these patterns persist, colleges and universities will continue to reproduce the social advantages of dominant groups instead of serving as engines of upward mobility (Leonhardt, 2004). The intent of this book is to draw attention to the unique experiences of working-class college students, reveal systems and structures that continue to create barriers for these students' access to and success in higher education, and develop a deeper understanding of how faculty and staff can work to ensure they experience smoother—and more success-ful—transitions to higher education and beyond.

Who Are Working-Class College Students?

Social class has both cultural and economic components. For this reason, I have chosen to use the term *working class* as opposed to *low-income students, students living in poverty,* or other terms that might reference only students' economic condition. Ryan and Sackrey (1984) described class as a "cultural network of shared values, meanings, and interactions" (p. 107). Certain expressive cultural practices can signify class membership—including manner of dress, standard or nonstandard uses of grammar, or accents. Thus, social class membership has sometimes been described as *performance* because institutionalized social structures create distinct classifications or groups whose members act out or display dif-ferences in their cultural expression (Bettie, 2000). Moreover, class membership shapes individual experiences as participants in a larger society. Lubrano (2004) offered the fol-lowing conceptualization of class and its influence on identity development:

> Class is a script, map, and guide. It tells us how to talk, how to dress, how to hold ourselves, how to eat, and how to socialize. It affects whom we marry; where we live; the friends we choose; the jobs we have; the vacations we take; the books we read; the movies we see; the restaurants we pick; how we decide to buy houses, carpets, furniture, and cars; where our kids are educated ... In short, class is nearly everything about you. And it dictates what to expect out of life and what the future should be. As powerful as it is ... class is intangible, a metaphor that marks your place in the world. It's invisible and inexact, but it has resonance and deep meaning. It's resilient, having retained shape and structure through the years. (p. 5)

Although there are common themes woven throughout working-class students' identities and experiences that signify their social class position, it is important not to interpret refer-ences to working-class students in this text as monolithic. That said, any discussion of this population and their needs, aspirations, and success relative to higher education demands some understanding of who they are. Several defining themes—parents' educational status, occupation, and socioeconomic status, in addition to students' race or ethnicity—are discussed in the following sections.

Parents' educational status. Many working-class students are the first in their families to attend college, and several researchers have either pointed out the correlations between working-class identification and first-generation status or relied upon first-generation status as a proxy for working-class status (Hurst, 2010, 2012; Lehmann, 2009; Rubin, 2012a; Stuber, 2011). There is a substantial amount of overlap between social class and parental education; for example, Soria (2012) found working-class students were four times more likely than middle- and upper-class students to be the first in their families to pursue a bachelor's degree. Education matters in our society, shaping one's economic and life trajectory in rather profound ways, and educational level is often a proxy for skill level or human capital (Teixeria & Abramowitz, 2008). The associations between social class and educational attainment of parents should not be overlooked when exploring the experiences of working-class college students.

Parents' occupation. The prestige of an occupation is nearly synonymous with income, education, and overall social standing, and occupation is a strong predictor of class identification (Gilbert, 2008). In the workplace, different groups of people are simultaneously connected to yet distinct from each other by the ways in which they interact with (or hold) power, suggesting class differences. Typically, working-class individuals hold lower status occupational positions in society with comparatively little power or authority, exercise limited control over the content of their work, labor under close supervision, and do not supervise others (Barratt, 2011; Teixeria & Abramowitz, 2008). Blue-collar positions (e.g., construction or factory workers) are often seen as low status, but many white-collar positions (e.g., technical, sales, clerical) are similarly low status. Working-class college students are more likely to have parents who hold lower status occupational positions. While parents' occupations are important markers of social class, the necessity of work is also an identifier of social class on campus, as working-class students are often required (or expected by parents) to be employed while enrolled in college (Schwartz, Donovan, & Guido-DiBrito, 2009).

Socioeconomic status. Remarking on the economic foundations of social class differences, Jensen (2012) noted, "if culture is the medium through which class inequality is recreated—the arms, hands, and legs of class—it is still economic power that is its spinal column—the core of class in America" (p. 29). Given that working-class students are more likely to have parents who did not earn a college degree and who work in less prestigious occupations, these students are more likely to come from families with lower incomes and fewer financial resources (Gilbert, 2008; Hurst, 2010; Soria & Barratt, 2012; Zweig, 2000). Illustrating this point, Soria and Barratt's (2012) study of more than 90,000 college students enrolled at 12 large, public research universities found that 93.4% of low-income students and 71.8% of working-class students reported family incomes below $65,000 per year, compared to 32.8% of middle-class, 10% of upper-middle-class, and 8% of wealthy students respectively. The $65,000 marker offers a measure of middle-class status as it falls between the median ($51,017) and mean ($71,274) overall household incomes in the United States in 2012 (U.S. Census Bureau, 2012). Furthermore, economists suggest middle class may refer to incomes ranging from $39,736 (the third quintile of household incomes; $39,736 to $64,553) to $104,087 (the top of the fourth quintile of household incomes; $64,554 to $104,087; Elwell, 2014).

Although often conflated with one another, it is difficult to draw a one-to-one correlation between social class and socioeconomic status (SES) or parental income for several reasons. First, social class tends to be more stable across generations than SES (Jones & Vagle, 2013), and it is possible for individuals working in blue-collar occupations to hold working-class identities and yet earn relatively high incomes (Rubin, Denson, Kilpatrick, Matthews, Stehlik, & Zyngier, 2014). Social class and SES also need to be considered within the context of co-occurring constructs, such as ethnicity or regionality (Rubin et al., 2014).

Intersections of race, ethnicity, and gender. The intersections of race, ethnicity, gender, and social class dynamically engage social identities through interwoven systems of hegemony and oppression in socially constructed spaces. Some have suggested that isolating the influence of any one social identity (e.g., gender, race, ethnicity, or social class) masks a deeper understanding of how membership in multiple identity groups can affect college students' experience of the campus environment, engagement in colleges and universities, and achievement of important institutional outcomes (Museus & Griffin, 2011).

There are undeniable connections between race and class in our society. According to Soto (2008), "discussing race without class analysis is like watching a bird fly without looking at the sky: it's possible, but it misses the larger context" (p. 12). In the United States, the historic connections between race, class, income, and upward mobility have significantly disadvantaged people of color. For instance, nearly two thirds of individuals living in poverty are from minority backgrounds (Engle & Tinto, 2008). Jehangir (2010) stressed that demographic differences manifest into interrelated systems of racism and classism within educational environments, which are also linked to other systems of historical inequity.

People of color face more unique challenges and burdens as they achieve upward mobility than White people who also advance up the social ladder, especially because people of color must navigate dominant, White cultural milieus in education and the workplace (Vallejo, 2012). The larger social inequities are difficult to overcome, as evidenced by rates of unemployment and poverty among Blacks and Hispanics (McNamee & Miller, Jr., 2014). Vallejo's (2012) research on socially mobile Mexican Americans, for example, suggested that upward mobility does not mean one can automatically reap the benefits associated with the White middle class, including accumulation of wealth or effortless negotiation of the social and business worlds. Instead, people of color often struggle to maintain interethnic relations with White people who do not perceive them to be bona fide members of the middle class.

While social classes may be evident among different racial and ethnic groups, class stratification also divides racial and ethnic populations. For instance, Winkle-Wagner (2009) found social class was a major taboo among the Black women in her study, who only talked about such issues when they knew that they were with others from similar social class backgrounds. Historically, class-based divisions have widened divides between Black Americans from lower and middle classes (Cole & Omari, 2003; Graham, 1999). However, being born with a middle-class status does not offer people of color the same degree of protection against downward social mobility as that offered to middle-class White Americans; instead, "the effects of racism continue to position middle-class Black people as 'outsiders' irrespective of their class position" (Rollock, Vincent, Gillborn, & Ball, 2012, p. 254).

The intersections between gender and social class are also of importance to scholars and practitioners. Perceptions of the roles of men and women in occupations, families, education, and society vary by social class. For instance, working-class men are often expected to conform to working-class norms of masculinity, which features "non-academic work, sports, a rejection of authority from schoolteachers, sexism, homophobia, misogynistic language" (Ward, 2014, p. 719) or pressures to become primary breadwinners and sources of stability for their families (Silva, 2012). While men are afforded many privileges in society due to their gender position, working-class men face significant challenges in their efforts to attain higher education and graduate. They may develop a hyper-masculinized and labor-focused identity to combat the emasculation they feel in not having power and privilege in society—an identity that lies in opposition to higher education, which they reject or resist because it is framed as too effeminate or esoteric (Archer, Pratt, & Phillips, 2001; Morris, 2005). Such an identity is, in many ways, antithetical to very traditional forms of higher education that feature intellectual, white-collar work activities and the ability to display middle- and upper-class forms of capital. Working-class men who attend college are thus tenuously positioned in a system that is simultaneously resisting—and being resisted by—them. Higher education institutions reject traditional masculine working-class worldviews and social customs, as they are viewed negatively in comparison to middle- and upper-class norms.

Working-class women often receive different messages regarding educational expectations that encourage them not to pursue higher education—the expectation to marry and have children (Evans, 2009; Matthys, 2013; Tett, 2000), for example. For many working-class women, the personal ambition to achieve higher education may be perceived as confrontational (i.e., against others) while it may be interpreted as part of the natural order (i.e., individualistic and for themselves) for working-class men (Evans, 2009; Tett, 2000). Working-class women who participate in higher education at the expense of starting families of their own or leaving their existing families behind often experience a sense of survival guilt—especially if their ability to attend college happens alongside the loss of family relations (Lucey, Melody, & Walkerdine, 2003; Tett, 2000). Lubrano (2004) found survival guilt is a common theme among working-class students. These findings are corroborated by other researchers who have reported working-class students (and women in particular) are more likely to live at home or visit home frequently while attending college, most often due to their close-knit ties or familial responsibilities (Abrahams & Ingram, 2013; Bryan & Simmons, 2009; Tett, 2000).

While women have rapidly closed educational gaps compared to men, the power structure of the United States remains dominated by men, and women are disproportionately employed in low-level occupations such as administrative assistants (96%), preschool and kindergarten teachers (97%), registered nurses (91%), and receptionists and information clerks (93%; U.S. Department of Labor, 2011). McNamee and Miller (2014) referred to this low-level job landscape as the "pink ghetto" because, while many of these jobs pay well and carry moderate prestige, they tend to be "order-takers" rather than "order-givers," have short mobility ladders with nonexistent promotions, and are located at the bottom of occupationally defined chain of command (p. 193). Socialized within the broader culture, working-class women may opt out of higher education or, if they do attend college, self-select degree programs that lead to pink-ghetto occupations.

Intersectionality theories promote an awareness of the implications of holding multiple identities; yet, social-class membership as a singular component of social identity exerts a powerful influence upon individuals, and class plays a stronger role as a barrier to college entrance—and a predictor of educational achievement—than race, ethnicity, or gender (Van Galen & Noblit, 2007). As a result, those who work in colleges and universities should remain attentive to the importance of social class in the development of students' complex intersected identities.

Self-identification of social class. Many factors influence self-identification or self-categorization with respect to social class. For example, membership in lower social classes tends to carry negative stereotypes, and individuals may avoid self-categorization in these groups to avoid stigmatization (Lott, 2002). Similarly, Gorman (2000) discovered working-class individuals tended to denigrate middle-class values and attitudes, claiming that the middle class looks down on others, puts their careers before family, and does not perform real work. Such strategies serve to maintain a positive collective self-evaluation of social class status. Yet, for working-class college students, these strategies cause discordance between the negative messages they may hear about middle-class lifestyles at home or in their communities and their middle-class pursuit of higher education.

As with other social groups, there is also the potential for members of low-status classes to attempt to pass as members of higher status social class groups. Poor and working-class students often adopt the speech patterns, dress, and other markers of middle- and upper-class status to fit in with their peers (Kuriloff & Reichert, 2003). While individuals from working-class backgrounds can acquire middle- and upper class cultural competencies, they can never achieve the natural facility of those born in the upper-classes; therefore, understanding class differences as cultural differences partly explains the anxiety and discomfort expressed by working-class academics who perceive they are only passing in middle-class academia (Heller, 2011; Muzzatti & Samarco, 2006; Schwartz et al., 2009). The salience of one's social class position may also become more or less prominent in specific situations. For example, class differences are typically made more salient for working-class students who attend universities where most students are middle- and upper-class. Working-class students may not openly divulge their class status in such environments, potentially preventing them from forming social bonds with students from similar backgrounds (Kuriloff & Reichert, 2003).

As students leave their families for college and are exposed to new belief systems, values, and lifestyles, relationships with friends and family often change. In addition to these challenges, working-class students must also renegotiate class identity (Baxter & Britton, 2001). These renegotiated identities often signal a distinct break or disconnection from family members and home communities, which may be especially true for first-generation students who feel as though they have developed two separate identities to navigate their college and home worlds (Bryan & Simmons, 2009).

Meritocratic Myths: Examining the Discourse of Social Mobility

The U.S. educational system is predicated upon principles of meritocracy. That is, more education leads to economic security and upward mobility. One of the underlying assumptions of the meritocratic myth is that social class is an individual endeavor (Jones & Vagle, 2013). As such, higher education is the "great social class equalizer" (Langhout, Rosselli, & Feinstein, 2007, p. 147), and individuals have full agency to design their own economic fortunes through the achievement of higher education. Wealth is also framed within terms of individual efforts (Ostrove & Cole, 2003)—if one simply works hard enough, one will be justly rewarded. Poverty is framed in opposite terms: It is because one is lazy or lacks ambition that one remains poor (Ostrove & Cole, 2003).

While attaining higher education certainly improves opportunities for social mobility, there is little evidence to suggest that we live fully within an education-based meritocracy, one in which obtaining a college degree wipes out the effects of social class origins on the probability of upward mobility (Goldthorpe & Jackson, 2008). Instead, one's social class at birth remains a rather stubborn predictor of social class in adulthood (Chetty, Hendren, Kline, Saez, & Turner, 2014). Despite the extent to which individuals attribute their upward mobility to their own efforts and abilities, one's family background exerts tremendous influence on future prospects, and the upper class is a position into which one is born (Bowles, Gintis, & Groves, 2005). Zweig (2000) noted the crucial role that luck plays in social mobility—"the most important piece of luck, good or bad, is the family you happen to be born into" (p. 46).

Upward mobility rates are scant at best and are significantly lower in the United States than in other industrialized countries (Norton & Ariely, 2001). In fact, intergenerational mobility remained stable for children born between 1971 and 1986, and income inequality has increased over time (Chetty et al., 2014). The analogy of social mobility offered by Chetty et al. is that of a ladder with each percentile representing a different rung. The rungs of the ladder have grown further apart over time as inequality has increased, although a child's chances of climbing from lower to higher rungs has not dramatically changed over time. The probability that a child with parents in the second quintile of income distribution (i.e., those who might be categorized as working class) would reach the top 20% of income distribution was 17.7% for children born in 1971, compared to 13.8% for children born in 1986. Strikingly, the authors also found that children born to the highest income families in 1984 and 1993 were 74.5% and 69.2%, respectively, more likely to attend college than children from the lowest income families.

Higher education can provide a path of upward mobility to some in the working class. In reality, however, the disproportionate rate of higher education attendance among working-class students when compared to middle- and upper-class students serves to stabilize classes and reproduce them across generations (Zweig, 2000). Even if higher education does forge channels for upward social mobility, the reverse—that a lack of higher education is matched by downward social mobility—has not been substantiated. In fact, scholars have found that those in the middle and upper classes maintain their social class standing at significantly higher rates than those in the working class (Goldthorpe & Jackson, 2008; Zweig, 2000). The important takeaway is that, contrary to popular opinion, social class in the United States is not an individual choice; instead, social class is veritably steeped in longstanding broad economic, social, and political contexts (Jones & Vagle, 2013).

Even among these harsh realities, however, the grand educational discourse maintains that "a good job, economic security, and upward mobility [are] waiting at the end of the credentialed rainbow" (Jones & Vagle, 2013, p. 131). Upward mobility in our society is not only culturally acceptable—it is a fundamental expectation of citizens. Correspondingly, downward social mobility and persistence in the working class appears anachronistic. The pressures to pursue upward mobility through higher education are deeply rooted in meritocratic ideals, yet these same pressures also signify that working-class students are inherently deficient or lacking due to their social-class position—a condition that can be repaired through higher education (MacKenzie, 1998). In turn, some working-class students may not possess the analytical framework to understand that their social-class position is rooted in structural inequalities and may, therefore, unwittingly adhere to meritocratic belief systems. Among successful students, these beliefs reinforce the idea that their hard work is paying off, and, for unsuccessful students, they serve as a reminder of individual deficiency (Aries, 2008; Twenge & Campbell, 2002).

Given the power of this narrative, social class is an uncomfortable theme in American society, and several scholars (e.g., hooks, 2000; Shor, 2005) have argued that most people in the United States are in heavy denial of the privileges that come with increased socioeconomic status. This denial has resulted in a dearth of research related to social class in U.S. higher education, although there has been a quiet emergence of such scholarship over the last decade (Schwartz et al., 2009). The majority of the literature published on working-class college students emanates from other countries—most commonly, the United Kingdom, Australia, and Canada. As a consequence, within U.S. higher education, matters of class are often overlooked and subsumed by discussions of race and ethnicity, leaving the unique class-based experiences of many students underrecognized and undertheorized (Pearce et al., 2008).

It is not my intention to subordinate the importance of race, ethnicity, or gender to social class; rather, my purpose is to draw a renewed focus and attention to social class because it is so often disregarded as an important element of college students' social identities and because it bears considerable weight on several aspects of the collegiate experiences and outcomes. Levine and Dean (2012) suggested social class is a "potentially more powerful issue than race, ethnicity, or gender because it builds on the current heterogeneity and cracks within those communities" (p. 115). Students' class identities are social constructions entangled in longstanding webs of structural inequality, yet these identities are complicated by meritocratic myths purporting that social class, at least in the United States, is an individual choice, and that everyone receives an equal opportunity for social advancement.

The Purpose of This Book

The goals of this book are to raise attention to the experiences of working-class college students amid a critique of the greater social class(ed) structures of higher education that have historically marginalized students from such backgrounds. It is widely acknowledged that working-class students' needs are unmet because their presence in colleges and universities is largely ignored (Barratt, 2011; Hurst, 2010; Kezar, 2011; Soria, 2012; Stuber, 2011; Walpole, 2007). Higher education institutions are almost "completely blind to working-class students, even while ignoring or tacitly silencing their voices" (MacKenzie, 1998, p. 96). Current modes of thinking about diversity in terms of the visible differences among college students persist in "glossing over certain forms of cultural differences, and continues, in an unreflective manner, to advance the middle-class ideology of the academy as the normative one" (Galligani Casey, 2005, p. 34). Given these gaps, one purpose of this book is to reveal aspects of the higher education system that both affirm and norm middle- and upper-class culture, thereby alienating working-class students who pursue higher education and pressuring them to conform to middle-class norms.

By discussing theories that expose how educational structures reproduce social classes; shedding light on the hidden class curriculum of higher education; and examining how that curriculum is enacted in the academic and social spaces of the campus, this book serves as a guide for higher education practitioners in reframing traditional deficit perspectives of working-class students. In addition to exposing institutional policies and practices that disenfranchise working-class college students and attribute failure to their individual characteristics, this volume provides constructive strategies for higher education practitioners to support this population. Social class remains an understudied topic in the higher education literature, especially scholarship written for practitioners. Consequently, this text offers new perspectives and insights into the class-based experiences of students in higher education in addition to specific steps practitioners can take to develop more inclusive environments for students from working-class backgrounds.

Chapter 2
THEORETICAL PERSPECTIVES ON SOCIAL CLASS IN HIGHER EDUCATION

In order to gain richer perspectives of the structural barriers facing working-class students, this chapter draws upon Bourdieu's (1996) explorations of the means by which social class is reproduced in society. Higher education research related to social class (Berger, 2000; Kezar, 2011; Lareau, 2003; Walpole, 2003, 2007) has relied heavily on this work. Bourdieu's theory of social reproduction can help practitioners understand some of the challenges facing working-class students as they transition to higher education.

Poststructuralism and Bourdieu's Theory of Social Reproduction

The predominant theoretical frameworks commonly used to understand social class in higher education emanate from poststructuralist traditions (Kezar, 2011; Walpole, 2007). Early poststructuralist theorists reacted against grand theories (e.g., Marxism) that suggested larger structures and systems determined human behavior and outcomes (e.g., one's social class position). While structuralists broadened awareness of obscured systems that reinforce social class, thereby revealing that social inequalities were not solely rooted in individual choices, poststructuralist perspectives emphasized the existence of human agency, resistance, and tension when individuals encounter the broader system (Kezar, 2011; Lareau, 2003).

Bourdieu identified patterns of domination and inequality in society and studied the strategies individuals use to maintain or improve their social positions (Lareau, 2003). Like other poststructuralists, Bourdieu suggested status and privilege are not earned by skills, effort, or intelligence; instead, individuals' social positions are a function of cultural experiences and socialization, which translate into different forms of capital as people advance through life (Crossley, 2008; Lareau, 2003). Bourdieu never offered a typology of social classes and rarely discussed the concept of class directly in his work (Crossley, 2008), suggesting instead that individuals are positioned in social spaces that influence their cultural skills, lifestyles, social connections, educational practices, and other cultural resources (Crossley, 2008). Bourdieu acknowledged the complexity and fluidity of social life: People possess varying skills, resources, and networks that they can use to their advantage throughout their lives, such as relying on social connections to obtain employment opportunities.

One of Bourdieu's greatest contributions to educational research is the notion that educational systems reproduce social classes by granting continued advantages to children from culturally (and economically) wealthy backgrounds who can successfully navigate those systems (Bourdieu & Passeron, 1977). The education system confers a great deal of value and prestige upon the culture of the middle class, which maintains its power by virtue of this attenuated legitimacy (Bourdieu, 1984; Bourdieu & Passeron, 1977). The dominant culture represented in higher education serves to reproduce the dispositions of those who already possess that culture, most often to the detriment of those who do not (Grenfell, 2004).

When social reproduction theory is applied to working-class college students, it can be broadly stated that these students are more likely to feel a cultural mismatch and a sense of alienation in an educational system that legitimizes and values middle-class culture. As a result, working-class college students often feel like they are living in a foreign land (Bryan & Simmons, 2009). To avoid feelings of alienation, these students may be less likely to enter into educational structures and, when they do, may be less successful (e.g., less likely to graduate) than their middle-class counterparts because the cultural and social capital of their upbringing is not rewarded in the college setting (Winkle-Wagner, 2009, 2010, 2012). This cycle perpetuates social class stratification in society, with the middle and upper classes continuously retaining power and privilege.

Of Bourdieu's prolific work, educational researchers have readily applied several key concepts: *field*, *habitus*, and *capital* (namely, cultural capital and social capital). The following sections provide greater insights into each of these concepts and how researchers have applied them in scholarship related to working-class college students.

Field

To understand human interactions or social phenomena, Bourdieu (1971, 1988, 2005) argued for examining the social space, or field, within which these interactions or events occurred. Bourdieu stated that social spaces can be stratified in key areas, and he devoted considerable time and attention to the educational field as a space that benefitted those who already possessed social and economic advantages. Some scholars have attended to the educational field and its role in reproducing social inequality, suggesting that the educational norms of the middle class are further reinforced because this ruling class in educational systems has the power to impose evaluation criteria deemed most favorable to the products of its own class (Bourdieu, 1984). In other words, middle-class students embody dispositions recognized and valued by teachers, who perceive these students to be "brighter and more articulate" because they "speak the same language" and possess cultural knowledge and abilities similar to those of the teachers (Crossley, 2008, p. 95). In contrast, some teachers tend to deride working-class students as having low intelligence or intellectual ability (Brantlinger, 2003; Espinoza, 2011; Jensen, 2012).

Social reproduction is not simply about whether working-class students bring the "right" social and cultural resources to campus; rather, it examines how the social and cultural resources interact differently in the specific contexts—the unique fields—in which students find themselves (Stuber, 2011). The organizational and ecological variations within higher education institutions may or may not programmatically exclude working-class students from the social and extracurricular domains of campus life (Stuber, 2011). For example, community colleges, regional universities, and public universities may be more welcoming to working-class students due to the opportunities they provide for these students (e.g., lower tuition, flexible schedules). Elite universities, prestigious research-oriented institutions, and liberal arts colleges may perpetuate class bias and reinforce class stratification because they present more symbolic and real barriers to working-class students (e.g., class bias, disparaging stereotypes and comments about working-class individuals, perceptions of inferiority, higher tuition, inflexible schedules; Astin & Oseguera, 2004; Bourdieu, 1988, 1996; Oldfield & Conant, 2001; Shott, 2006).

College campuses often have different social-class cultures due to the composition of students and faculty and the institutional mission (Barratt, 2011). For example, regional branch campuses may have a lower social class culture than main campuses, and community colleges may have a lower social class culture than four-year institutions. Working-class students who attend regional institutions face much less class discrimination than students who attend more elite institutions (Christopher, 2003); however, like underresourced primary and secondary schools in low-income neighborhoods, regional institutions receive far fewer resources than the more elite main campuses (Christopher, 2003; Linkon, 2008). Faculty who work at regional and community colleges often teach classes with large enrollments and have more advisees, meaning that they have less time to provide each student with individual support. While human resources at these types of colleges are strapped, it is also the case that students and faculty at regional colleges and universities across the nation take classes and work in "run-down buildings and lack access to technology, materials, and staff support" (Linkon, 2008, p. 10). Working-class institutions, much like working-class college students, are at once invisible, marginalized, and denigrated because they "don't fit the standard image of college" and are considered "second-rate schools" (Linkon, 2008, p. 10). Thus, working-class students who attend regional colleges and universities receive an impoverished version of higher education because these institutions lack access to the types of resources more readily found at prestigious institutions (e.g., well-stocked libraries, high-quality facilities, new technology; Linkon, 2008).

Working-class students may be more likely to enroll in nonelite institutions in part due to their feelings of familiarity with those institutional contexts but also because low-cost vocational education is more appealing and comfortable to some working-class students (Goldhaber & Peri, 2007; Lehmann, 2007; Lippincott & German, 2007; Reay, Davies,

David, & Ball, 2001). Ironically, the decision to attend community colleges or open-access institutions may serve only to reinforce social reproduction of the class system, as these types of institutions have lower graduation rates than more selective institutions (Carnevale & Rose, 2004; Karabel, 2005). Furthermore, because the value of a degree often rests heavily upon the class, prestige, and status of an institution, graduates from regional, two-year, or open-access institutions are not as likely as their peers who graduated from elite universities to receive good jobs or access to graduate programs (Linkon, 2008).

Habitus

An additional influence on the reproduction of social class is one's class environment or habitus, a "common set of subjective perceptions held by all members of the same group or class that shapes an individual's expectations, attitudes, and aspirations" (Bourdieu, 1986, p. 9). Habitus is both structured and structuring—it is structured by one's past and present experiences (e.g., family upbringing) and structuring as it shapes one's present and future practices, behaviors, and perceptions. Habitus focuses on individuals' ways of thinking, feeling, acting, and being and how, as they develop, young people reproduce the dominant cultural habitus of their upbringing.

Early discussions of habitus in social reproduction theory addressed why middle-class individuals were more likely than those from working-class backgrounds to participate in higher education. Bourdieu and Passeron (1977, 1979) noted that middle-class individuals see higher education as a natural step in their life trajectories—as part of their inheritance— more often than those from lower social classes. They may also feel more at home while attending college because the unwritten rules of the game were internalized as a part of their socialization and conditioning in the middle-class habitus (Lareau, 2003; Maton, 2008). Working-class students, on the other hand, encounter challenges fitting into the middle-class habitus of higher education because they are cultural outsiders, a position which contributes to feelings of inadequacy (Aries & Seider, 2005; Granfield, 1991; Lehmann, 2004). Such feelings often compromise working-class students' decisions to stay enrolled in higher education despite their strong academic performance, suggesting the presence of unreconciled discontinuities between working-class students' habitus and the middle-class habitus of higher education (Lehmann, 2007). The historical domination of middle-class groups in educational institutions has therefore positioned higher education as alien to working-class groups.

In describing the tensions working-class students have in their newfound middle-class habitus, several authors have identified strategies that students are likely to take to reconcile habitus—including decisions to withdraw. Quinn (2004) described the dropout decisions of working-class students as a form of loyalty to their culture. Similarly, the working-class students in Lehmann's (2007) study suggested they felt more at home and had a greater sense of comfort when they dropped out of their universities and pursued apprenticeships or vocationally oriented training programs. Working-class students who enter higher education make an initial break with the sociostructural confines of their working-class habitus, interpret their experiences while enrolled through the lens of their upbringing, and make decisions to withdraw because their college experiences do not reinforce the sociocultural norms with which they are most familiar (Lehmann, 2007).

These challenges compromise working-class students' sense of belonging and integration, thus contributing to their lower persistence and graduation rates (Aries & Seider, 2005; Granfield, 1991; Lehmann, 2007; Ostrove, 2003; Ostrove & Cole, 2003); however, given that Bourdieu's theory emphasizes individual agency, it is possible for working-class college students to adopt elements of the middle-class habitus through improvisation (McDonough, Ventresca, & Outcault, 2000; Walpole, 2007). Hurst (2010) described those working-class college students who resisted acculturation into the middle class as *loyalists* and those who tried to acquire cultural capital and spent much of their time emulating their middle-class peers as *renegades. Double agents* are those who can move between both working-class and middle-class cultures. Hurst (2010) found that loyalists are much less likely to advance economically and materially than renegades, although renegades and double agents carry many emotional burdens as a consequence of forsaking their social class habitus of upbringing and living between worlds of inferiority and superiority (Baxter & Britton, 2001; Lehmann, 2013; Lubrano, 2004; Stuber, 2011).

Capital

Bourdieu (1986) distinguished between economic capital (i.e., accumulated money or wealth) and symbolic forms of capital, including social capital (i.e., network of acquaintances) and cultural capital (i.e., knowledge or familiarity with the dominant culture). There is little doubt that economic capital impacts students' decisions to enroll in higher education, which college to attend, and the constellation of activities pursuant to engaging in the college environment (see Chapter 3). Yet, social and cultural capital play an equally important role in all these areas as well (Stuber, 2011). Researchers have turned much of their attention to the cultural and social capital of working-class students, which are described in more detail in the sections that follow.

Cultural capital. This is a broad concept—often considered to encompass verbal facility, highbrow aesthetic preferences, educational credentials, and knowledge of educational systems. Bourdieu (1997) distinguished between three kinds of cultural capital: (a) *embodied cultural capital,* cultivated dispositions acquired through socialization; (b) *objectified cultural capital,* material objects that require embodied cultural capital to appreciate (e.g., works of art); and, (c) *institutionalized cultural capital,* most often acquired through academic qualifications. McNamee and Miller (2014) described cultural capital as "a set of cultural credentials that certify eligibility for membership in status-conferring social groups. To 'fit in' and 'look and know the part' is to possess cultural capital" (p. 77).

Cultural capital has been operationalized as knowledge of high-culture, participation in high-culture events (e.g., attending an opera or the ballet) and the arts; consumption patterns and monthly expenditures; educational attainment; possession of high-culture goods, including art and books; and accumulated knowledge of education in the family system (Langhout et al., 2007; St. John, Hu, & Fisher, 2011; Sullivan, 2001; Zimdars, Sullivan, & Heath, 2009). Cultural capital reflects a system of interrelated factors not easily isolated from one another (Zimdars et al., 2009).

Cultural preferences for elite or highbrow activities perpetuate social distinctions, which serve to dominate people. Bourdieu and Wacquant (1992) termed this "symbolic violence" (p. 170)—people are "dominated in and through these social distinctions but they may not realize it or they may accept it as natural and fair" (Winkle-Wagner, 2010, p. 15). These cultural preferences, according to Horvat (2001), are accepted without recognition as an exercise of power and are instead viewed as a part of the natural social order. Cultural capital serves as a means of distinguishing and continuously defining social classes, and it is accumulated through socialization, although the possession of cultural capital is often (falsely) perceived to be based on individual merit (McNamee & Miller, 2014). Advancement in society is facilitated by the acquisition of relevant skills, knowledge, attitudes, tastes, and competencies privileged by the dominant classes (Bourdieu, 1984; Bourdieu & Passeron, 1979; Winkle-Wagner, 2010)—in other words, cultural capital.

Researchers point to three ways in which parents influence their children's acquisition of cultural capital: Children may acquire it (a) by living in homes where parents possess prestigious cultural capital, (b) by spending time in their friends' homes within a similar or higher social strata, and (c) by engaging in activities thoughtfully and strategically managed by parents to transmit prestigious forms of cultural capital (Mohr & DiMaggio, 1995). Those means of acquiring cultural capital are relatively "frictionless," whereas, acquiring cultural capital from the outside—such as through higher education—"is a much more daunting and difficult task" (McNamee & Miller, 2014, p. 87). Lareau's (2003) ethnographic work on the childrearing practices of middle- and working-class families demonstrated significant differences between the types of cultural capital cultivated. Middle-class parents were intentional in finding and providing experiences to actively develop their children's social, intellectual, and physical capabilities—leading middle-class children to feel more comfortable navigating dominant social institutions. However, working-class parents were more likely to allow their children to engage in free play and other unstructured activities. Lareau argued that these childrearing practices play a role in social reproduction because working-class children received little socialization regarding how to interact in dominant social institutions. Stuber (2011) speculated that exposure to these class-based styles of socialization differentially prepares college students to interact with peers, professors, and broader higher education institutions, leaving middle-class students more confident engaging with others in higher education than their working-class peers.

Social capital. Distinct from cultural capital, social capital was defined by Bourdieu and Wacquant (1992) as "the sum of the resources, actual or virtual, that accrue to an individual or a group by virtue of possessing a durable network of more or less institutionalized relationships of mutual acquaintance and recognition" (p. 119). Social capital provides opportunities for one to draw upon resources from other members of the networks to which he or she belongs. Bourdieu (1986) and Coleman (1988) argued that social capital influences the social and economic well-being of individuals. Although Bourdieu perceived social capital as an individual possession, Coleman acknowledged that it existed within networks and communities and had value for all communities, including marginalized groups (Horvat, 2001; Walpole, 2007). Putnam (2001) described social capital as "social networks and associated norms of reciprocity" (p. 21) and noted the private and public benefits of social capital: Well-connected individuals in poorly connected communities do not fare as well as well-connected individuals in well-connected communities.

College students' socioeconomic background contributes to the formation of their social capital—a process that begins even at very early stages of life. For instance, Lareau (2003) noted that working-class children have fewer structured interactions with peers and professionals than middle- and upper-class children who are purposefully placed in environments and activities that increase their social capital and provide them with knowledge to generate future social capital. Based on Lareau's work, it is often acknowledged that working-class students lack "sufficient social capital networks to succeed in higher education" (Gupton, Castelo-Rodriguez, Martinez, & Quintanar, 2009, p. 250). Whereas middle-class students benefit from family or school-based networks for academic support, working-class students do not possess the same networks and therefore do not reap the benefits of social capital, including knowledge about going to college, navigating college, and understanding how to receive financial assistance (Stanton-Salazar, 1997; Winkle-Wagner, 2012).

Academic capital. Recently, some critics have advocated advances in Bourdieu's theory when it comes to application in the field of higher education. For example, Barratt's (2007) addition of academic capital—the knowledge and skills necessary to be successful in school—considers the influences of educational culture prior to higher education. Within that perspective, it is relatively easy to imagine that parents who have earned college degrees are more likely to transmit academic capital (e.g., how to study, where to study, what classes to take while in college, what majors to pursue) to their college-bound students than are parents with no college experience.

Closely related to this, academic capital formation theory considers several capital theories at once—human capital (i.e., the economic value to be attained by personal investment in higher education), social capital, and cultural capital (Winkle-Wagner, 2012). The theoretical claims of academic capital formation are that attending college is more than just acquiring skills or knowledge (human capital); instead, college attendance is linked to social networks (social capital) and developing social and cultural competencies (cultural capital) that can lead to generational uplift and advances in social status. Access to higher education is much more than just the ability to afford tuition; instead, students need emotional, social, and academic support to navigate the hidden pathways to college success (Winkle-Wagner, 2012).

Conclusion

Higher education institutions are predominantly designed by—and for—those in the dominant middle class; consequently, working-class students face several barriers as they enter colleges and universities. This chapter has outlined several frameworks for understanding the challenges facing working-class students in higher education. The next chapter delves a bit deeper into the structural barriers working-class students encounter in the education system and continues the critical analysis of the theories described in this chapter.

Chapter 3
ACCESS TO HIGHER EDUCATION: EXAMINING THE ROOTS OF DISPARITIES IN ATTENDANCE AND ATTAINMENT

The myth of meritocracy suggests that social class is an individual endeavor or choice rather than something that is structurally reproduced across generations. For working-class students, this means facing immense pressure to attend college, which is frequently regarded as an important step toward achieving upward social mobility. At the same time, they are expected to enroll in postsecondary education and succeed even amid the structural barriers they encounter. These barries include systematic differences in their preparation for higher education, encounters with discrimination while enrolled in college, and challenges to their social class identities. In reality, these structural barriers result in lower retention and graduation rates for working-class students. This chapter describes the roots of these barriers.

Precollege Academic Experiences

Working-class students experience significant structural disadvantages with regards to their precollege academic preparation, such as limited enrollment in rigorous high school courses; lower scores on entrance exams, such as the ACT or SAT; less preparation for college-level academic work; and fewer qualifications for admissions at four-year institutions (Choy, 2002; Engle, 2007; Haveman & Smeeding, 2006; Horn & Nunez, 2000; Soria & Barratt, 2012; Stuber, 2011; Terenzini, Cabrera, & Bernal, 2001; Warburton, Bugarin, & Nunez, 2001). A recent study found only 9% of first-generation students across the nation met college preparation benchmarks in all four subject areas of English, reading, science, and math (ACT and Council for Opportunity in Education, 2013). In many cases, low-income and minority students do not have access to the best courses and teachers and, even in schools that are diverse, minority students are often segregated in classrooms that meet lower educational standards (Oakes, 2008; Oakes & Saunders, 2008).

Evidence suggests that students are more likely to succeed academically in higher education if they take rigorous courses—including foreign languages, upper-level writing, and math—as early as the seventh and eighth grades (Fullinwider & Lichtenberg, 2004). Math courses are especially important in promoting the success rates of college students. When low-income, first-generation, and students of color take advanced math courses in high school and aspire to higher education, they not only attend college at the same rate as White students but also succeed in higher education at equivalent rates (Adelman, 1995, 2005; Choy, 2002). Adelman's (2003) research demonstrated that a strong math background essentially trumps socioeconomic advantages: Each quintile increase in students' SES background increased the odds of graduating by 1.68:1, but each quintile rise in math accomplishment increased the odds by 2.59:1. However, students from low-income backgrounds are significantly less likely than their peers to have access to advanced math courses (St. John & Chung, 2007). They are also less likely than their upper-class peers to have written research or analytical papers, enrolled in foreign language classes, received feedback on their writing skills, or enrolled in Advanced Placement (AP) classes (Aries, 2008). Some working-class students have even described their high school courses as being so nonrigorous that they did not require them "to think" (Aries, 2008, p. 155).

Working-class students are more likely to be placed into general or vocational education tracks than college preparation tracks and have fewer academic, social, and financial resources—all of which negatively affect their aspirations for, enrollment in, and success in higher education (Adelman, 2006; Aries, 2008; Engle & Lynch, 2011; Paulsen & St. John, 2002; Sacks, 2007). They are also less likely to receive encouragement from their high school counselors and teachers regarding college attendance (Horn & Nunez, 2000), and students who characterized their interactions with guidance counselors as unhelpful and impersonal were less likely to enter college immediately after high school graduation (Johnson, Rochkind, Ott, & DuPont, 2010). High school counseling is especially critical for first-generation students whose parents have less knowledge about the college-going process and who may receive most of their college-related information from guidance counselors (Terenzini et al., 2001).

Yet, the students who would benefit most from access to good high school counseling may not receive it. High schools in affluent neighborhoods with greater financial resources create more favorable conditions to prepare students for college through smaller counselor-to-student ratios, enabling counselors to get to know students individually and prescreen them as potential applicants for different types of colleges and universities (Stevens, 2007). In addition to guidance counselors, middle-class students receive substantial support for the college-going process from parents, test preparation services, and tutors (Kahlenberg, 2010; Stevens, 2007). While affluent middle-class and upper-class students' transition from high school to college is well-supported by a "seamless web of interdependencies" between guidance counselors and admissions offices (Stevens, 2007, p. 247), working-class students receive significantly less support in the transition to college.

As such, students from working-class backgrounds are much less likely to take college placement tests than their upper-income peers are (Pallais & Turner, 2007; Terenzini et al., 2001), a factor that could be a product of limited precollege counseling. Factors such as apathetic teachers, being pushed out of the college academic track, decreased access to counseling and guidance, and fewer educational resources form a vicious cycle for working-class students. They become disengaged from educational systems and do not consider postsecondary education, in turn, reinforcing teachers' and counselors' beliefs that working-class students are a poor fit for higher education due to their disengagement and lack of interest in college (Hurst, 2012).

Moreover, significant disparities exist in working-class students' high school graduation rates. In 2009, the dropout rate for students living in low-income families was about five times greater than the rate of their peers from high-income families (7.4% vs. 1.4%) (Chapman, Laird, Ifill, & Kewal Ramani, 2011). High school success and graduation is important in facilitating students' enrollment in higher education, as many colleges and universities consider the diploma (or equivalent) and high school grade point average as requirements for admission. Consequently, due to lower secondary school success rates, students from working-class backgrounds are disproportionately disadvantaged with regards to their eligibility to attend colleges and universities.

Finally, some of the systems surrounding college admissions structurally disadvantage working-class students. Because of cultural bias in the SAT college entrance exam, critics suggest that it has become a "vicious sorter of young people by class" (Sacks, 2001, p. 7). Citing evidence of strong, positive relationships between SAT scores and family income, several authors have suggested that the SAT exam preserves privilege and economic inequality through its class bias (Fullinwider & Lichtenberg, 2004; Guinier & Sturm, 2001; Sacks, 1999). Overwhelming evidence shows precollege academic preparation is critical to college students' access and success (Perna & Hadinger, 2012); working-class students are therefore more likely to feel the negative effects of these inequalities while in transition to higher education. Even among students with similar test scores, high academic achievement, and class ranks—and from identical schools—those from higher-income families are significantly more likely than those from lower-income families to attend college, particularly four-year colleges (Kane, 2004; McDonough, 1997).

The College Choice Process

In the United States, admission to elite colleges is often based upon extracurricular activities, personal characteristics, and sometimes athletic ability (Stampnitzky, 2006). The class-based understanding and valuing of dominant class character and personality qualities (i.e., cultural capital) for admissions allows colleges and universities to attract, admit, graduate, and (re)produce society's elite classes (Stampnitzky, 2006). Cultural capital has been used in higher education research as a way to explore the college choice process and access (McDonough, 1997), admission to elite universities (Zimdars, et al., 2009), the transition to college (Walpole, 2003), and student retention (Berger, 2000), among other areas.

Working-class students are less likely to attend college—particularly four-year colleges and universities—than their middle-class peers (Astin & Oseguera, 2004; Engle & O'Brien, 2007; McDonough, 1997; Tinto, 2006; Walpole, 2007). Despite programmatic changes, access rates for working-class students have dropped while rates among middle-class students have risen over the last 30 years (Bowen, Chingos, & McPherson, 2009). Haveman and Wilson (2007) found an almost 50-point percentage gap in college attendance between students in the top and bottom economic quartiles. In 2004, only 43% of students from families with incomes under $30,000 entered higher education immediately after high school graduation, compared to 75% of students from families with incomes above $50,000 (Long, 2008).

While disparities exist among students' decisions to enroll in higher education, inequalities also affect *where* students choose to attend college. Working-class students are far more likely to choose two-year and for-profit colleges than four-year colleges and universities (Choy, 2001; Engle & Tinto, 2008; Hurst, 2012; McDonough, 1997; Paulsen & St. John, 2002). When they do enroll in four-year institutions, those schools are likely to be less competitive. Among 146 top-tier colleges and universities, 74% of the entering class came from the highest socioeconomic quartile, 10% from the bottom half of the socioeconomic distribution, and only 3% from the lowest socioeconomic quartile (Carnevale & Rose, 2004). The disparity continues at less selective schools. Carnevale and Rose (2004) found a 39-point gap in tier-two schools and 25- and 19-point gaps in tier-three and tier-four schools, respectively. Several additional scholars have demonstrated that access to selective institutions has decreased for low SES students over the last several decades (Astin & Oseguera, 2004; Karabel, 2005; Tinto, 2006). Working-class individuals are just as likely to attend an Ivy League school today as they were in the 1950s, suggesting little has changed with regard to access to elite forms of higher education for this populaion (Karabel, 2005).

The current structuring of admissions criteria may be partially to blame for this gap. Working-class students who attend high schools with fewer college-going students are structurally disadvantaged because many elite colleges and universities use the percentage of high school graduates from each applicant's school who continue directly on to four-year colleges as an evaluation criteria—the assumption being that a higher percentage means a more rigorous college preparatory and academically oriented school culture (Stevens, 2007).

Prestigious higher education institutions also require more than academic accomplishment for admission. These institutions place a premium on extracurricular activities or athletic abilities on top of enrollment in Advanced Placement or honors courses in high school (Stevens, 2007). Middle-class parents more adequately prepare their children to meet those desirable admissions criteria by making a series of decisions (some even before children are born) with an eye toward college, such as purchasing more expensive property in communities with good schools, starting college funds and savings accounts, securing slots in prestigious private schools as early as kindergarten, enrolling their children in college preparatory courses, shuttling their children to and from competitions and structured activities, and investing concertedly in the development of their children's extracurricular abilities (Lareau, 2003; Ornstein, 2007; Stevens, 2007).

Stevens (2007) critiqued the middle-class system of child development and its corresponding values, suggesting they were firmly intertwined with the system of elite higher education—so much so that the "system that the elite colleges and universities developed to evaluate the best and the brightest is now the template for what counts as ideal child rearing in America" (p. 247). However, this child development process is difficult for families with modest incomes to emulate. Thus, the system of higher education is falsely advertised as meritocratic when indeed it reinforces—and is reinforced by—middle- and upper-class social systems. The interdependence between privileged families and elite higher education institutions results in an entering first-year class that represents "the product of an elaborate organizational machinery" (Stevens, 2007, p. 247) whose upper tiers were conscientiously designed to send elite colleges the right candidates, while the function of those elite colleges, in turn, is to certify the upper tiers as the most accomplished or deserving of their status. Bourdieu's (1996) theories of social reproduction strongly resonate with these ideas and suggest that, in addition to being a *stratified* system, higher education is, thus, also a *stratifying* system because highly selective institutions have greater rates of persistence and graduation, provide access to elite graduate programs, and are associated with high-status career tracks and increased economic earnings (Astin & Oseguera, 2004; Bowen et al., 2009; Carnevale & Rose, 2004; Karabel, 2005). The opportunities that reinforce social class status for students from wealthier backgrounds are not afforded to students from lower socioeconomic backgrounds, who may stand to benefit the most from such opportunities; thus, social class inequalities are reproduced (Bourdieu, 1996).

The college choice process is significantly different for working-class college students. Given their lesser college-going knowledge, lack of support, and fewer educational and financial resources, they are more likely to choose a college by chance or serendipity (Reay, David, & Ball, 2005), because of its proximity to their home (Hurst, 2012; Stuber, 2011), and for the financial aid offers (Stuber, 2011). Some of these factors also stray beyond the college choice process to the selection of a college major. Although working-class parents are emotionally supportive of their children, those who did not attend college possess limited knowledge about higher education and are therefore unable to help with many aspects of the college-going process, including choosing a major—unless the major choice is framed in occupational terms (Aries, 2008; Bryan & Simmons, 2009; Matthys, 2013). Working-class parents often encourage their children to see college as preparation for work and are not often able to help students cope when they encounter challenges while enrolled in higher educa- tion (Longwell-Grice, 2003). As a consequence, the process of deciding upon an academic major has been described as "a series of trial and error" for many working-class students who do not receive parental assistance in selecting their academic pathways (Matthys, 2013).

Admissions Policies

Researchers have also described the ways in which working-class students are disad- vantaged by early-decision or early-action practices, legacy admissions, admissions based on athletic prowess, and merit awards—all opportunities that disproportionately benefit students from upper-class backgrounds (Bowen, Kurzweil, & Tobin, 2005; Fullinwider & Lichtenberg, 2004; Kahlenberg, 2010; Karabel, 2005; Stevens, 2007). The contemporary justification for legacy admissions policies is that they positively impact alumni giving, yet Coffman, O'Neil, and Starr (2010) found evidence that contradicted this perception. After controlling for institutional characteristics (e.g., size, control) and the demographic profiles of alumni (e.g., median midlife earnings) and incoming students (e.g., the percentage of students receiving Pell grants), the authors found no evidence suggesting legacy preference policies exerted any influence on alumni giving behavior.

Early-decision programs require students to apply early for admission, usually in November, and, in return for a decision in December, students promise to enroll. Early- action programs work similarly but are nonbinding with regard to enrollment. Fullinwider and Lichtenberg (2004) contended that early-action and early-decision programs advantage affluent students because they are more likely to have better information about colleges and are more likely to have spent time visiting colleges and universities than working-class students. Students who are admitted early tend to receive less financial aid because they are "locked in" and "colleges have no incentive to win their favor" (Fullinwider & Lichtenberg, 2004, p. 88). However, these options are not favorable to working-class students who are more dependent upon financial aid packages. Working-class students who apply and are admitted through early-decision programs may forsake more sizable financial aid packages from other institutions.

Financial Factors

It nearly goes without saying that many working-class college students also struggle with issues concerning financial aid and the overall affordability of higher education. For instance, working-class students are more likely than their peers to believe that a college education is not financially feasible (Tierney & Venegas, 2009) and to have unmet need not covered by financial aid (Choy & Carroll, 2003). After taking financial assistance, such as student loans or grants into consideration, working-class students and their families spend on average 25%-40% of their annual household income paying for college, compared to middle- and upper-income families, who spend approximately 1%-7% of their annual income on college expenses (Lott & Bullock, 2007). Research suggests that lower-income college students with unmet financial need are forced to choose "levels of enrollment and financing alternatives not conducive to academic success, persistence, and, ultimately, degree completion at any institutional type" (Advisory Committee on Student Financial Assistance, 2001, p. 10).

Working-class students who attend colleges and universities predominantly pay for education by taking out loans or working (usually full time)—especially if they lack financial assistance from their family members (Hurst, 2012). Some of the students in Hurst's (2012) study could not report their parents' financial information because they were estranged; others felt an incredible sense of guilt going to college because they were no longer contributing to their family financially; and a number of other working-class students could not ask their parents for any financial assistance because there was simply no money to give. Hurst (2012) described one student who became emotional when his father gave him $20 on his first day of college:

> How little it was, how much it meant, how impossible it would be to explain this gesture to anyone else he met at college, for by this time Michael knew that his story was not the same as the others he saw emerging from the shiny cars with neat crates and boxes full of their adolescent belongings, parents in tow. (p. 56)

Dickert-Conlin and Rubinstein (2007) noted that "financial aid and college costs cannot and do not account for most of the inequality in higher education processes or outcomes" (p. 2); instead, working-class students face a network of barriers, rather than a single observable one, in their pursuit of higher education (Chambers & Deller, 2001). These networked barriers are symbolic of the class-based hierarchical system that oppresses working-class students and reproduces societal privilege and power (Bourdieu, 1997). Furthermore, the financial decisions made by working-class students while enrolled in higher education can compromise their academic experiences, serve as a disruptive barrier to success, delay or prolong graduation, or increase their debt. For example, Soria, Weiner, and Lu (2014) discovered working-class students were significantly more likely than middle- and upper-class students to assume credit card and loan debt, work more hours, and take a leave of absence to manage the financial costs of college attendance.

College Success and Postgraduation Outcomes

Persistent inequalities follow working-class students from admission to graduation—inequalities that are symbolic of a hierarchical social system that reinforces the power of the middle and upper classes. Working-class students are less likely to persist, graduate from college, and attend graduate school than their more advantaged peers (Ishitani, 2006; Terenzini et al., 2001; Walpole, 2003). The disparities in degree attainment levels between social classes have only accelerated over time: Mortenson (2010) noted that students born into the top quartile of family income were 10 times more likely to earn a baccalaureate degree by the age of 24 than students in the bottom quartile. In 2008, the difference was nine times; in 2007, the difference was eight times; and, going back to 1980, the difference in graduation rates between students in the upper and lower quartiles of family income was five times (Mortenson, 2010). At prestigious institutions, the statistics are even more startling: Students from families in the 99th percentile of income are 25 times more likely to graduate from highly selective colleges than their peers from low-income backgrounds (Karabel, 2005).

Working-class students are significantly more likely to experience interruptions in their postsecondary educational pursuits. College students from low SES backgrounds had nearly three times the odds of stopping out of one school and moving among schools with interruptions, which can be attributed to their academic and financial struggles (Goldrick-Rab, 2006). The disparities in degree attainment rates between students from lower and higher social-class backgrounds continue to perpetuate class differences, causing greater "gaps between the 'haves' and 'have nots'" (Dickbert-Conlin & Rubenstein, 2007, p. 1) and denying students from lower-income families the "richness of opportunities provided the children of inherited privilege" (Mortenson, 2010, p. 1).

Where students choose to enroll initially may have an adverse impact on their chances of degree attainment. Working-class students are more likely to enter two-year than four-year institutions, and students who attend community colleges with the intent of transferring to four-year colleges are less successful than those who attend four-year institutions immediately after high school graduation (Leigh & Gill, 2003). While many believe two-year colleges can provide working-class students with opportunities to launch their academic careers so they can transfer to four-year institutions, higher-income students who attend community colleges are more likely to transfer successfully than low-income students (Dougherty & Kienzl, 2006). For example, Balz and Esten (1998) found only 1.5% of low-income first-generation college students who attended community colleges finished a bachelor's degree in five years. It is well established that the economic returns of a bachelor's degree far outweigh those of associate degrees (Goldhaber & Peri, 2007); consequently, working-class students who do not complete their bachelor's degrees may lose out on the economic advantages of college attendance.

These disparities also extend to students' postgraduation outcomes. Working-class students are more likely to seek degrees with limited or short-term upward mobility, to attend college to further their employment opportunities, to be channeled into fields with clear career prospects (e.g., nursing, or teaching), and to be employed in vocationally oriented fields following college graduation (Goyette & Mullen, 2006; J.E. King, 2005; C.S. King, 2012; Paulsen & St. John, 2002). These patterns are also found within more prestigious institutions where low-income students were more likely to select majors affiliated with teaching or counseling careers, occupations that would not reach the same level of income or power as the occupations selected by their peers from wealthier backgrounds (e.g., law, medicine, or business; Seider, 2008).

Additionally, working-class students are much less likely to persist to graduate school. The disproportionate representation of high SES students gives them a long-term advantage for high-status jobs and greater income than the low SES students who earned vocationally oriented degrees (Goyette & Mullen, 2006). The differences between low and high SES students persist beyond graduation. Nine years after entering college, students from low SES backgrounds reported lower levels of income, graduate school attendance, and educational attainment than peers from higher SES backgrounds (Walpole, 2003). Working-class college students are much less likely to pursue doctoral education and face substantially greater challenges in financing such education, they incur higher levels of debt, and they take longer to graduate (NORC, 2007).

Conclusion

As this chapter has demonstrated, working-class college students face significant challenges on the path to higher education—structural barriers and obstacles that make the chances of achieving success that much more unlikely. Even those who make it to college face an uncertain future. They are much less likely to graduate and face less robust career prospects than their middle- and upper-class peers. The next two chapters examine the academic and social experiences of working-class college students and explore how these experiences contribute to a diminished set of outcomes.

Chapter 4
CLASS IN THE CLASS(ED)ROOM

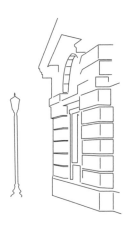

As noted previously, many working-class students enter higher education with lower levels of academic achievement than their peers, including lower high school grade point averages and standardized test scores. While enrolled in college, working-class students are also more likely to have lower cumulative grade point averages than middle- and upper-class students (Aries, 2008; Soria & Stebleton, 2013; Terenzini et al., 2001; Walpole, 2003). An overriding conclusion in the literature is that social class is positively associated with academic performance and retention, with working-class students less likely to be academically successful than their peers (Robbins et al., 2004). This chapter outlines some of the factors underlying working-class students' level of academic achievement in higher education contexts, including the cultural messages about education and intelligence that working-class students encounter, the hidden curriculum of higher education that privileges the middle class, and structural barriers to working-class students' success. The chapter concludes with a discussion of pedagogical strategies aimed at overcoming some of these disadvantages.

Cultural Messages About the Working Class

Many stereotypes of working-class individuals are based on the perception that they are less intelligent than people from middle- and upper-class backgrounds (Hurst, 2010). Such stereotypes allege that working-class individuals are naturally fit for subordinate occupational and social positions due to their lower intelligence (MacKenzie, 1998). Consequently, college students whose parents' occupations are of a manual rather than a mental nature are devalued in educational circles (Hurst, 2010; Rose, 2004) and haunted "by the clinging, deep-rooted suggestion that their class identity is a badge of cognitive failure" (MacKenzie, 1998, p. 100).

These misconceptions carry over into students' experiences in higher education, where working-class students often encounter lower expectations from faculty, many of whom assume these students will lack intelligence (Christopher, 1993; Plummer, 2000)—a perception confirmed by the fact that working-class students are more likely to report faculty do not take them seriously (Aries, 2008). Middle-class students frequently take the initiative and seek to develop rapport with faculty—often because they know relationships with faculty grant access to other privileges and opportunities (Smith, 2013). Working-class students, on the other hand, perceive college faculty and administrators as gatekeepers whose role it is to make education more challenging (Longwell-Grice, 2003) and who intentionally put up roadblocks to test them (Longwell-Grice & Longwell-Grice, 2007-2008). They some-times experience college faculty as indifferent or overtly hostile toward them (Longwell-Grice, 2003) and may believe that faculty do not value their academic work as much as that produced by middle-class students (Warnock & Appel, 2012). Classrooms become, for many working-class students, sites of symbolic violence in which class-based notions of education and intelligence mark them as inherently less capable than middle-class students (Charlesworth, 2000). Perhaps not surprisingly, working-class students were reluctant to speak with faculty outside class (Longwell-Grice & Longwell-Grice, 2007-2008). Hurst (2012) noted that the intimidation factor combined with hectic work schedules makes it difficult for working-class students to interact with faculty beyond the classroom. Working-class students often suffer in silence because they do not want to give the impression they are unintelligent and do not belong in college. As a result, they miss out on opportunities to build social capital with their professors (Smith, 2013).

Working-class students also encounter lower expectations from their peers. For instance, a student interviewed in Hurst's (2012) study remarked that classmates were uncomfortable including him in groups and did not provide him opportunities to contribute. He became so exasperated one day that he stopped his group's conversation and exclaimed, "Hey! I'm right here! Can't you see me?" The sense of invisibility he felt has been echoed by other working-class students (see Hess, 2007).

Working-class status may create stigma for some students, but others find they inhabit a world in which their social-class position—and corresponding class-based experi-ences—are largely ignored by others. For example, when a former truck driver enrolled in college provided a personal example of a family member living on public assistance in an economically distressed community, classmates "cringed" and there seemed to be "an embarrassed silence in class" (Hurst, 2012, p. 73). The professor barely acknowledged the story, leaving the students in the classroom to deduce that "telling stories about your life were not appropriate in the college classroom" (Hurst, 2012, p. 73) unless they conformed to the middle-class narrative. Such experiences may lead working-class students to actively avoid getting into classroom-based conversations about poverty or welfare because of the embarrassment they believe may emerge from these discussions (Hurst, 2012). Similarly, students may purge their assignments of any personal information, writing themselves "completely out of the page" (Hurst, 2012, p. 77).

Because middle-class college students are the majority on many four-year campuses, faculty and administrators may presume that all students share similar class origins, cultural backgrounds, and perspectives (Hart & Hubbard, 2010). As a consequence, class-blind prejudices, where social class is not acknowledged as a relevant factor in explaining cultural differences (Heller, 2011), are likely to emerge. For example, faculty and staff may assume all students have similar ability to pay for books and course materials; access to technology, such as computers and printing; and available free time for studying and completing homework (Hart & Hubbard, 2010). The reality is that many working-class students struggle to pay for books and course materials, do not have access to technological resources, and may spend a significant amount of time working. As a result, they may find it difficult to engage fully in their educational pursuits and even self-select out of higher education altogether.

The negative messages working-class students receive about intelligence and education sometimes originate at home. For example, in working-class families and communities, street smarts are privileged over book smarts, a sign of resistance to an educational system that has left them behind. For working-class college students, being book smart is a "taboo of sorts," and even the most intelligent are plagued by a constant fear of being humiliated in college (Matthys, 2013, p. 200). Thinking they are being protective of their children, many working-class parents send messages to their children to lower their ambitions, behave according to their current class position, "know their place" in society, and not set their sights too high with regard to education (Matthys, 2013). Working-class students receive conflicting messages—their parents may encourage them to pursue higher education, although the very act of achieving higher education and entering the middle class undermines (or renders inferior) parents' own working-class identities. Matthys (2013) suggested the messages of anti-intellectualism mean that working-class students who choose higher education are essentially excommunicated in a symbolic sense from full working-class cultural membership.

Due to their social subordination and the cultural messages working-class students receive promoting anti-intellectualism, some may be resistant to higher education (Martin, 2008). Lindquist (2002) explored this resistance and suggested education represents a disassociation from working-class interests in which those attending higher education are perceived as actively distancing themselves from—and thereby implicitly *devaluing*—the working class. These tensions have been described elsewhere in this text. Working-class students enrolled in higher education have bought into society's message that a college education is a ticket to the middle class. To make the journey to the middle class means breaking away from the values of their upbringing. As such, schools become like battlegrounds—sites of symbolic oppression in which working-class students are compelled to conform to middle-class ways of being just to survive.

Hidden Curriculum

The "hidden curriculum" of higher education—the norms, values, beliefs, and processes of socialization that students learn but are not overtly taught—reproduces social inequalities in subtle ways. Saturated with middle- and upper-class cultural capital, the hidden curriculum serves to maintain the predominance of the middle and upper classes over the working class. For instance, the hidden curriculum teaches students about inequality as status quo—some students are naturally more intelligent or work harder than others and therefore gain greater status and rewards. The hidden curriculum also teaches competition and normalizes the creation of hierarchies based on what are often perceived to be cognitive attributes (e.g., honors programs, dean's lists). Thus, the hidden curriculum reinforces myths of meritocracy and solidifies beliefs that those in the middle class are entitled to their academic successes.

Another aspect of the hidden curriculum includes knowing the types of information that can help students be more successful as they apply for and enroll in college, such as knowing which books to read in preparation for college (e.g., the great books constituting the Western Canon), the types of experiences one should have while in college (e.g., traveling for spring break), and how to interact with faculty on any number of issues or concerns (e.g., asking for an extension on an assignment). Middle- and upper-class students possess greater knowledge about these higher education processes that enables them, before they even enroll, to develop clear academic goals, identify college pathways for achieving their goals, and engage in strategies to accomplish their academic pursuits (Armstrong & Hamilton, 2013).

The cultural capital possessed by the middle and upper classes constitutes the invisible curriculum in higher education and, in order to achieve success, working-class students "must learn to adopt and represent middle-class culture as one's own" (Jensen, 2012, p. 156). Middle-class students are culturally advantaged in these systems because of the norms of their upbringing. While middle-class parents perceive themselves as greater or equal to their children's teachers and actively intervene on behalf of their children, working-class parents are more likely to assume that the teachers know best and, thus, are less likely to intervene (Calarco, 2014). These parents' beliefs and attitudes toward education may trickle down to their children. For instance, middle-class students are more likely to advocate for themselves and ask for help, whereas working-class students are reluctant to ask for help when they are struggling (Calarco, 2014). As a consequence of their upbringing, middle-class college students may feel much more comfortable engaging in challenging conversations with faculty, whereas working-class students may not challenge these authority figures (McLoughlin, 2012). Similarly, working-class students are not accustomed to critiquing author's claims and sharing their own ideas (McLoughlin, 2012)—symptoms, perhaps, of feeling an overall lack of agency and voice when it comes to intellectual matters.

Scholars have investigated the connections between class-based socialization of children at home and their subsequent performance in—and familiarity with—systems of education. Through imitating their families, middle-class children develop into adults who "learn the rules of the game that enable them to negotiate with authorities and make the rules work in their favor" (Jensen, 2012, p. 86). These rules, at least in higher education, become a part of the hidden curriculum for working-class students—the unspoken rules that working-class students are expected to follow without explicit knowledge of them. For example, the hidden curriculum teaches students about independence and individualism—that schoolwork is, by and large, an individual responsibility not shared with others. These independent models of learning and performance are more congruent with middle-class students' expectations of higher education and do not match with the interdependent models more often found in working-class communities (Stephens, Townsend, Markus, & Phillips, 2012). In fact, Stephens et al. developed an experiment in which first-generation students were asked to read hypothetical university welcome letters—one of which emphasized a university culture of independence and self-sufficiency (e.g., learning by personal exploration, creating one's own intellectual journey) and another which emphasized interdependence (e.g., learning by being a part of a community, connecting to fellow students and faculty). The researchers discovered increases in markers of stress and negative emotions in first-generation students who read the letter emphasizing a culture of independence. They suggested the stress first-generation students experienced could be attributed to a cultural mismatch between expectations for independence rather than interdependence.

A focus on independent effort typically emphasized in university cultures minimizes the value of community-based academic efforts, ignores social inequalities, and places the blame on individuals if they are unsuccessful. Those who are able to reach the top of the academic ladder do so by virtue of their own personal abilities. These lessons indoctrinate obedience to capitalistic norms and values which, for working-class students, justifies their lower social status because they are taught to view any academic failure or even slight academic mediocrity as a result of their own personal inadequacies—rather than a symptom of capitalism's need to maintain a hierarchical workforce, including low-wage and low-status blue-collar laborers (Chapman, 2004).

The hidden curriculum of higher education, left unrevealed to students, "disables working-class students. For, without the kinds of connections that come with privilege, [working-class] students need to learn an arsenal of strategies" to help them achieve academic success in higher education (DeSalvo, 1998, p. 18). Schwartz et al. (2009) stressed that the unwritten expectations of higher education need clear, explicit articulation for nondominant groups unfamiliar with its elite culture, yet the challenge is that current systems in higher education "hide" available resources from working-class students. Hart and Hubbard (2010) found, for example, that in order to benefit from resources, including financial support for health care, winter coats, discounts and waivers for books, and free eyeglasses, students enrolled at a women's college were expected to know how to navigate the system to access those resources and were forced to disclose their social-class background to receive support. The expectation that working-class students should know how to navigate the system on their own reflects a lack of critical awareness of the experiences of these students. Ultimately, Hart and Hubbard (2010) contended that the system reinforces institutional power at the expense of students who have less power.

Structural Barriers to Academic Success in Higher Education

There are several structural barriers preventing working-class students from achieving the same degree of academic success as their middle-class peers, and it is important to understand that these obstacles are not attributable to individual student characteristics. Instead, such inequalities are rooted within the K-12 educational system. Given that the education system reflects middle-class values, norms, and culture, working-class students' best efforts in their own cultural systems "do not translate easily—or sometimes at all— into the skills that schools require and reward" (Jensen, 2012, p. 115). Because they possess different forms of cultural capital than their middle-class peers, working-class students are less confident in their academic abilities, more confused by faculty expectations for assignments, and often less likely to seek help from faculty (Collier & Morgan, 2008; Jenkins, Miyazke, & Janosik, 2009).

Working-class students perceive that their peers from higher-income families are better conditioned to engage in the academic rigor of college and that they are at a structural disadvantage as a consequence (McLoughlin, 2012). They often avoid enrolling in difficult college courses, feel frustrated because they lag behind their peers, and experience a sense of stress at not being able to maintain the academic pace of their peers (McLoughlin, 2012).

They are also less likely to engage in the kinds of academic behaviors that might support their success. Some working-class students do not complete reading or course assignments on time, complain about academic workloads, avoid speaking with faculty unless it is to make last-ditch attempts to rectify grades, have spotty attendance, or withdraw from courses (Galligani Casey, 2005; Martin, 2008). Similarly, Terenzini et al. (2001) discovered that low-income students were much less likely to be involved in coursework activities, including taking notes, participating in class discussions, completing additional readings on course topics, and explaining course materials to friends or fellow students. The authors also found that lower-income students were significantly less likely to join study groups and meet with advisors for academic planning. Soria and Stebleton (2012) found, after controlling for additional demographic variables and college experiences, that first-generation students were significantly less likely to interact with faculty, make comments, bring up ideas from different courses, and ask insightful questions during class discussions. Lack of appropriate spaces for study and inadequate preparation for college-level work (e.g., poor study skills and behaviors) are obstacles to working-class students' academic success (Soria, Stebleton, & Huesman, 2013-2014) and may explain their lack of engagement.

Additional obstacles compromise working-class students' academic achievements in higher education; for example, many working-class college students report spending less time studying due to their family and job responsibilities (Soria et al., 2013-2014; Terenzini et al., 2001; Walpole, 2003). Others have also found working-class students have financial burdens, domestic conflicts, and caretaking responsibilities that may prevent them from attending class and completing assignments regularly (Grassi, Armon, & Bulmahn Barker, 2008). Students from working-class backgrounds work more hours while in enrolled in college and are more likely to work off campus than their middle-class peers (Armstrong & Hamilton, 2013; Cooke, Barkham, Audin, Bradley, & Davy, 2004; Terenzini et al., 2001; Walpole, 2003). Choy (2001) estimated that 70% of first-generation students are employed while enrolled in college. While work experience can benefit students by providing "valuable knowledge … regarding the world of work and social capital that can be converted to letters of recommendation from supervisors for jobs after graduation" (Walpole, 2003, p. 55), time dedicated to work activities often means less time for academic pursuits. The value provided by employment experiences may also depend on the nature of the employment. That is, working-class college students in blue-collar jobs probably will not acquire middle-class cultural and social capital through those roles.

Given that the majority of working-class students are required to be employed to fund their education and expenses, they may "forgo necessary sleep, relaxation, or recreation in order to survive financially and academically" (Martin, 2008, p. 36). This "habitual self-denial" may cause students to resent their academic studies, leading to further disengagement (p. 36). Combined with estrangement from peers and disconnection from faculty, in addition to parents who do not understand their experiences in higher education, working-class students may become further isolated as they attempt to engage in their academic pursuits alone.

Finances and academic achievement are precariously intertwined for working-class students. While high-impact educational practices are exceedingly beneficial, (Kuh, 2008), the costs for some put them out of reach for working-class students. These students are less likely to study abroad and participate in internships than their peers (Aries, 2008; Armstrong & Hamilton, 2013; Stuber, 2011). Scholarship programs to participate in study abroad, leadership opportunities, or unpaid internships can go a long way in supporting working-class students' engagement in high-impact educational experiences. Hidden costs of participation in some high-impact practices (e.g., access to a professional wardrobe) may also present barriers for working-class students. The University of South Carolina (2015) recently announced a new student government initiative, Carolina Closet, that will provide low-cost rental of professional attire for job and internship interviews. Programs that offer opportunities for employment—such as employment while studying abroad—may also present the means for working-class students to earn wages to support their daily needs (such as housing, meals, and recreation).

If working-class students transfer into their respective colleges or universities, they may miss out on opportunities to take first-year seminars or enroll in learning communities. For example, Soria (2013a) found transfer students at public colleges and universities were up to half as likely to engage in those types of high-impact practices traditionally found in students' first year. Finley and McNair's (2013) comprehensive study indicated that first-generation students participated in significantly fewer high-impact practices than students who are not first-generation. These missed opportunities have significant consequences for first-generation students, as they stand to benefit even more than other students from their participation in high-impact practices. In fact, first-generation students who participate in high-impact practices report deeper learning and greater gains in general education, practical competence, and personal and social development than their later-generation peers (Finley & McNair, 2013).

Strategies for Transforming the Classroom Learning Experience

The common thread running through college students' experiences is the engagement in learning activities, most of which are traditionally enacted within formal classroom spaces. Classrooms embody potent venues within which higher education institutions can reconfigure their systems to support working-class students. Approaches for practitioners to analyze institutional class structures and make social class more prominent in the classroom are discussed in the sections that follow. Additionally, methods are described to redress imbalances in the essential types of cultural capital working-class students need to be successful in higher education, suggestions are offered to honor students' identities, and steps are provided to develop communities within which working-class students may feel validated.

Making Class Visible

As noted elsewhere in this volume, the predominance of middle-class values and culture in higher education tends to make class differences invisible. The presence of faculty from working-class backgrounds—especially when they openly identify as working-class or first-generation and integrate their personal experiences in classroom spaces (Godinez Ballón, Chávez, Gómez, & Mizumoto Posey, 2006; Vander Putten, 2001)—can be a powerful counterbalance to the prevailing norms. Faculty can also discuss their own personal struggles to achieve mastery in their academic discipline as a way of closing the social and intellectual distance between themselves and their students (Morales, 2014). Their personal expressions of "humility and hardship" can help working-class students "buy into the possibilities of their own successes" (Morales, 2014, p. 96). While traditional forms of higher education represent, to working-class students, a foreign habitus, connections to faculty who have also felt like foreigners can make students feel more at home.

Yet, faculty from working-class backgrounds are likely to be underrepresented on many campuses. In this case, faculty from middle-class backgrounds need to engage in the work of making class visible. This means first learning to be reflective about the ways in which their middle-class worldviews calcify their position in social-class hierarchy (Vagle & Jones, 2012). Faculty who reflect upon, question, and disrupt their own ways of knowing and being are better positioned to develop class-sensitive perceptivity—to recognize when class is at play in their interactions with students. Vagle and Jones (2012) suggested faculty engage in intentional work around reframing their assumptions about others from different social-class backgrounds. For instance, the authors encouraged faculty to avoid thinking and saying that their students are "just lazy" when they do not read assigned texts and instead to try to think and say, "my students do not seem interested in what I have assigned—I need to ask them what they would like to read and do everything I can to get those materials in my classroom" (Vagle & Jones, 2012, p. 335). This suggestion resonates with the needs of working-class college students, who may be more engaged when readings and assignments are perceived to be relevant to their lived experiences.

Critical pedagogy (discussed in more detail below) can be an important tool for middle-class faculty, as it recognizes "the isolation and marginalization" of students based on race, ethnicity, gender, or social class can "shape their learning experiences" (Jehangir, 2010, p. 55). Ongoing professional development for new and seasoned faculty should embed critical pedagogies to help them gain these perspectives, acknowledge their own positions of power, and seek to construct opportunities to intentionally disrupt patterns of marginalization for the working-class students on their campuses.

Analyzing Existing Class Structures and Their Impact on Students

Reflecting on class-based worldviews and perspectives does not end with faculty; students also need to be engaged in the process of analyzing class structures and their impact. Critical pedagogies provide a theoretical foundation for understanding the "educational contexts of historically marginalized students" and can be "particularly germane" to working-class students (Jehangir, 2010, p. 54). Such approaches acknowledge, confront, and challenge systems of power and privilege, with the recognition that educational settings and curricula are not value-neutral but are instead sites of ongoing oppression and reproduction of power and privilege (Jehangir, 2010). For educators serving working-class students, an initial step is to help them become aware of the systems of social reproduction (Bourdieu, 1984) and the meritocracy myths framing educational attainment in our society.

Readings, films, or multimedia resources related to social class in the United States are valuable tools for exploring social and economic inequalities and their relationship to educational disparities. *The New York Times* (2005), for example, developed an interactive website featuring graphics, reports, and essays, along with a companion book, for its *Class Matters* series. The Public Broadcasting Service (2011) developed a companion website—including curricular materials—for the documentary *People Like Us: Social Class in America* (Alvarez & Kolker, 2001). The Center for Working-Class Studies at Youngstown State University (n.d.) is also a useful repository of readings, syllabi, videos, and curricular materials for teaching about social class in higher education. Similarly, Class Action (2014) offers abundant resources, including an extensive bibliography, lists of films, articles written by first-generation and working-class students, and a wealth of other materials that can be easily incorporated into classrooms.

Analyzing social class structures may also allow working-class students to reframe the challenges experienced in higher education as a function of structural systems of oppression rather than their individual characteristics (or perceived personal deficiencies). Research suggests that such reframing may lead to greater success in higher education for underrepresented student groups. For example, Stephens, Hamedani, and Destin (2014) conducted a randomized experiment in which first-year students were assigned to one of two conditions. In the control condition, senior panelists shared strategies for succeeding in college but none of their background information. In the intervention group, however, panelists shared background-specific information, including their parents' educational attainment, as they framed their suggestions for success. First-generation students who were explicitly provided information related to social-class differences had significantly easier transitions to college, were more likely to seek out campus resources, and were better able to overcome background-specific obstacles to success than peers who did not receive such information (Stephens et al., 2014).

Explaining the Rules of the Hidden Curriculum

Making class visible and analyzing class structures help minimize some of the negative impact on students, but these strategies do very little to dismantle those structures. Students may be more aware of the structures shaping their experiences, but they must still learn to function inside them. Because faculty and professional staff on college campuses are embedded within the systems of higher education, they have unique access to the knowledge or cultural capital working-class students need to succeed. Stephens et al. (2014) noted that many first-generation students lack insights into why they are struggling and do not understand how they can make improvements precisely because higher education practitioners seldom acknowledge the impact of social class on their educational experiences. For those students not embedded in cultures of power, "being told explicitly the rules of that culture makes acquiring power easier" (Delpit, 1995, p. 111). Examples of these rules in higher education may include study questions for reading assignments, detailed rubrics, and explicit guidelines for completing assignments. However, if faculty assume all students come from a middle-class background, they may neglect to communicate this information to their students. As such, faculty should be encouraged to design their courses using principles similar to those of universal design (UD), which holds that accommodations made for one group of users are likely to benefit all users (Higbee & Goff, 2008).

Faculty can also take small steps, like placing required texts and readings on reserve in campus learning centers or libraries, to make their classes more affordable for students (Langhout et al., 2007). Recognizing that students from working-class backgrounds may not feel authorized to contribute to class discussion, faculty may call on individual students rather than waiting for volunteers. Culver (2012) commented on the effectiveness of cold-calling: "many students who had never previously contributed to class discussions revealed themselves to be well prepared, as though they had simply been waiting for permission to speak." Faculty can also commit to serve as formal mentors for working-class students (Smith, 2013). Smith recommended that faculty mentors seeking to connect with students possess cultural sensitivity, flexible thinking, and competent communication skills. In return, protégés should be attentive, committed for the long term, and open-minded. Smith suggested that these mentor relationships revolve around frequent face-to-face meetings to facilitate difficult discussions and focus on advising (transmitting information and guidance), advocacy (using the mentor's social capital to benefit the student), and apprenticeship (working to empower students to advocate for themselves). Institutions can enable faculty to develop these mentorship relationships through formal structures; for example, faculty can be delegated funding to share meals with students, receive course load reductions to allow more time for mentorship, and work in tandem with other campus professionals to identify mentees who may be a good match based upon their similar interests.

Honoring Students' Lived Experiences

Because working-class culture is largely absent from higher education, students who are not middle class may feel like they and their experiences are invisible, at best. As such, opportunities to draw on their own culture and experience within the context of their academic study can be an especially validating experience. For example, Morales (2014) described the deep sense of satisfaction a student experienced when she was allowed to analyze rap lyrics in a poetry class. The student related that she "didn't mind doing the work because I chose it, it was mine … I worked harder on that paper than on anything I have ever done in school, and I'm also the most proud of it" (Morales, 2014, p. 97). Students' choice of the assignment led to greater feelings of ownership, which also encouraged more effort, engagement, and personal responsibility for task completion. Morales described such an approach as empowering students to view their academic competence in terms of a growth mindset as opposed to a fixed, innate intelligence. In other words, students learned they were excelling because of the amount of effort they put into their work and overcame the notion that they lacked the native intelligence to achieve certain academic outcomes. With the growth mindset, these working-class students felt a greater sense of self-efficacy.

According to Godinez Ballón et al. (2006), allowing students to incorporate their identities and experiences into all aspects of classrooms promotes cultural enrichment and creates tangible connections to greater social constructs in ways that affirm students' unique identities:

> The ability to produce text, to stand in the position of subject and tell one's story is central to our humanity. It is crucial that our students recognize themselves in history. Seeing your reflection in the course material is empowering, especially when these lived experiences are contextualized in economic and political terms. Making these connections between our individual life experiences and broader social processes is an important pedagogical strategy in developing critical thinking not solely as an abstracted analysis, but as a reflective process grounded in the experiences of every day. (p. 602)

While Zandy (1998) pushed for the inclusion of texts about working-class people in college classes, she acknowledged the challenge of placing their experiences "at the center of study rather than at the margins of a syllabus or not on the page at all" (p. 295). First-year seminars are excellent spaces in which to assign common readings involving working-class narratives, autobiographies of working-class individuals, and historical inequalities between social classes in America. As working-class students transition into career fields, capstone courses are also ideal places for them to examine their personal histories, expectations, and anxieties for their upcoming transitions. These spaces are also fertile ground in which students can explore their social class through autoethnographies, autobiographical reflections considered from critical perspectives (Green, 2003).

Creating Community in the Classroom

Working-class students thrive when classes are community-based, with group activities and rewards for collective efforts (Kezar, 2011). Furthermore, given that working-class students may be intimidated by faculty, community-focused learning experiences featuring collaborative and collective approaches to pedagogy can help them become more empowered in higher education. Faculty can create spaces that foster a sense of community in their classrooms, which can in turn serve as a rich source of cultural capital for working-class students. Johnson, Johnson, and Smith (1998) offered five strategies to build cooperative learning communities in classes: (a) structure positive interdependence among students, (b) require that students be held individually accountable for their work, (c) ensure students promote each other's successes in face-to-face meetings, (d) teach students how to work in teams by building their interpersonal and small-group skills, and (e) ensure students receive opportunities to engage in group-based reflections in which they can process their learning together. Students can also take an active leadership role in helping to create a sense of community among their peers by being coached to offer hospitality and openly express gratitude for the gifts of others in the classroom, among other practices (Block, 2008). Formally going around the room and acknowledging the unique talents and contributions of all students can help working-class students to feel affirmed in the classroom.

Conclusion

Jensen (2012) noted, "far from blossoming or thriving in school, working-class kids all too often merely *survive*" (p. 115). This chapter offered a snapshot of the academic experiences of working-class students in higher education. It is evident that the academic arena presents a point of friction for working-class students—the cultural messages they receive growing up foster an anti-intellectual perspective, and they must cut ties (at least, symbolically) with their familial and cultural traditions to pursue higher education. Yet for many students, the classroom is the primary point of contact with higher education. As such, the chapter also included suggestions for making the classroom a more welcoming space for working-class students. While this discussion explicated many of the academic challenges facing working-class students, the following chapter describes their social experiences in higher education.

Chapter 5
SOCIAL CLASS AND INTEGRATION ON CAMPUS

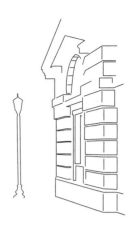

Several researchers point to the significance of students' social experiences in promoting their educational aspirations, persistence, and degree attainment (Astin, 1993; Tinto, 1993; Pascarella & Terenzini, 2005). Yet middle- and upper-class students may be better positioned to reap the benefits of peer interactions than students from working-class backgrounds. Students from advantaged backgrounds are more likely to have parents and friends who also attended college, a factor that renders the college-going experience more comfortable for them (Cooke et al., 2004). According to Stuber (2011), they have absorbed important aspects of cultural capital of the privileged class. They are "comfortable while on display and hav[e] the ability to talk to strangers, give them a firm handshake, and look them in the eye" (p. 71). Working-class students, on the other hand, struggle with establishing meaningful social relationships on campus (Lippincott & German, 2007)—perhaps, because they do not see themselves as having much in common with their classmates (Armstrong & Hamilton, 2013; McLoughlin, 2012). They are more likely to feel alienated at college, as though they are "marred by a painful sense of never quite measuring up" (Armstrong & Hamilton, 2013, p. 119). These experiences can even leave working-class students feeling so isolated that they consider transferring before their peers even get to know them (Armstrong & Hamilton, 2013).

As such, social experiences cannot be ignored for their benefits—nor can they be overlooked as potential sites of alienation and marginalization. This chapter addresses some of the obstacles to working-class students' social integration on campus. It is important to note that the classroom is a significant source of peer-to-peer interaction. Indeed, for some students, it may be the primary site of peer engagement. For this reason, discussions of social integration bridge curricular and cocurricular spaces within higher education.

Experiencing, Perceiving, and Understanding Social Class in College

Baxter and Britton (2001) suggested that lower-income students who participate in higher education are on a "trajectory of class mobility" (p. 99). As people move between social classes, their identities and relationships change, creating challenges in reconciling their acquired social class with the one of their upbringing (Aries & Seider, 2005). Having one foot in both the working- and middle-class worlds, while not fully belonging to either, may result in a deep sense of loss and a tenuous sense of belonging (Christopher, 2002; Wilson, 2002). Some students may experience "a painful dislocation from the former self, former relationships and affiliations, and former class identification" (Baxter & Britton, 2001, p. 99). Other scholars have documented alienation (Ostrove, 2003; Ostrove & Cole, 2003), estrangement and emotional dissonance (Stuber, 2011), feelings of subordination and chronic social anxiety (Matthys, 2013), burnout (Stuber, 2011), and isolation (Martin, 2012) as accompanying upward social mobility.

Because the college culture does not "grant dual citizenship" (Jensen, 2004, p. 178), working-class students are expected to conform to middle-class norms. Yet, attempting to negotiate this culture may leave working-class students feeling like imposters, which Daniels (1998) described this way: "I felt like I had scammed everybody ... and that at some point, the 'class police' would show up, inspect my credentials, and give me the boot" (p. 2). Closely associated with the imposter syndrome, class-jumping may also lead students to feel a sense of shame or embarrassment (Hurst, 2010). Ryan and Sackrey (1984) described the unrelenting fear working-class students face of being discovered and subsequently humiliated among their middle-class peers.

In higher education, students *learn to class*—to act middle class, to appreciate middle-class values, and to adhere to middle-class norms. Yet, the way college students experience, perceive, and understand social class depends on their felt or ascribed class status and that of their peers. Stuber (2006) discovered that clear "differences emerged between working- and upper-middle-class students in their class awareness, their class consciousness, and the kinds of symbolic boundaries they draw" (p. 294). Although there were similarities in how working-class and middle-class students talked about social class, less privileged students claimed to see class differences more clearly. Additionally, students from lower-income families were more sensitive to class issues and were more willing to believe that social class mattered. For example, Schwartz et al. (2009) noted the students in their sample—Mexican male college students—were able to clearly articulate their astute awareness of class in society and the university environment by identifying cultural rules and symbols associated with various levels of social class. Aries and Seider (2005) found the students who attended a private college reported greater feelings of inadequacy, intimidation, exclusion, and inferiority than those who attended the public state college. That is, they were more conscious of their social class in comparison to their more affluent peers. However, for the lower-income and first-generation students attending the public college, class-based differences were less salient.

Similarly, although many of the working-class students in Hurst's (2012) study could pass as middle-class—some because it was hip to wear thrift store clothes and take public transportation—most felt very different from their peers because of their background and attempted to actively hide their social class. Such stories are very common—working-class students discipline themselves to hide any traces of their class origins and contribute to their own "silence and invisibility" (Sullivan, 2003, p. 58). Working-class students also hide their accents or mimic the speech patterns of middle-class students; change their clothing, hairstyles, and accessories to fit in with their upper-class peers; consciously adjust their posture and mannerisms; intentionally misrepresent their social-class background; and do not disclose details about their families, especially their parents and their employment positions (Abrahams & Ingram, 2013; Aries, 2008; Hurst, 2012; Sullivan, 2003).

The potential for feelings of alienation and imposture can follow students into the workforce and professional education as well. For instance, the working-class law students in Granfield's (1991) study experienced a crisis in competency during their first semester. They reported significantly higher levels of stress and anxiety stemming from fears of academic inadequacy. Furthermore, they felt like cultural outsiders and often adapted to the middle-class culture of law school by concealing their social class, disengaging from their backgrounds to avoid feeling discredited by upper-class peers, and imitating middle- and upper-class culture. Granfield reported that students felt burdened because of their deception and often felt guilty because they believed they had sold out their own social class.

Working-class students have identified several critical incidents that spurred them to realize the economic and cultural differences between social classes on their campuses. For example, they often believe that their fellow students and university staff lack awareness of the issues and realities facing working-class students and feel as though stereotypical views of the working class were prevalent on campus (Hess, 2007). Awareness of social class differences may be more salient on specific occasions in higher education, such as when students first arrive on campus. The material possessions students bring with them to campus are clear markers of social class (Aries, 2008; Hurst, 2010; Stuber, 2011). Similarly, the ability to participate in certain social or extracurricular activities can make class positions more salient to students (Aries, 2008; Hurst, 2010). Working-class students may become more attuned to class differences when their wealthier peers travel abroad, go on extended trips, or take unpaid internships during school breaks (Aries, 2008; Armstrong & Hamilton, 2013). These students may adopt a false front as they struggle to put a positive spin on their emotions and labor to suppress their more complex negative reactions about their social-class experiences in higher education (Stuber, 2011).

While the transitions to higher education are uncomfortable for many working-class students, the very act of attending college helps students acquire new forms of cultural capital (Aries & Seider, 2005; Sullivan, 2003). For instance, working-class students in Aries's (2008) study reflected that they developed greater self-assurance in interacting with people from higher social-class backgrounds, including engaging in small talk; interacting with faculty and administrators; adopting a more intellectual worldview; and acquiring new tastes, preferences, and ambitions that distanced many from their families and communities of origin.

Lacking significant economic capital also hinders working-class students' social integration on campus. For example, working-class students often hold major work commitments that prohibit them from engaging in social interactions outside the classroom (Armstrong & Hamilton, 2013; Hurst, 2010). Yet, employment opportunities on campus may support social integration for working-class students and help them build important connections with their peers. Armstrong and Hamilton (2013) found that peer networks among working-class students were more likely to be located within work settings, whether on- or off-campus. Others (Kulm & Cramer, 2006; Soria, 2013c) have observed that student employment is positively associated with students' out-of-class social interactions with peers and their engagement in extracurricular activities. Students who work—especially on campus—may find that doing so provides them with opportunities to stay continuously connected to and persist on campus (Kulm & Cramer, 2006). Because many working-class students must hold a job while in college, it is important to let them know about on-campus employment opportunities well in advance of their enrollment so that they can secure these positions rather than seeking work elsewhere.

At the same time, practitioners should be aware of the potential for employment positions to reinforce lower-class status. The students in Hart and Hubbard's (2010) study described how social-class stratification was perpetuated by on-campus work-study positions. The students from lower social classes had jobs, such as dishwashers and housekeepers in their on-campus residences, which reinforced their social-class markers and propagated hierarchical class-based differences among their peers. The working-class students in Armstrong and Hamilton's (2013) study felt like second-class citizens who performed service for economically advantaged students. Similarly, Lubrano (2004) described the deep resentment he had toward his middle-class peers because he had to work a "menial job" to afford tuition (p. 76). Practitioners should therefore be mindful of the types of student employment opportunities they create, as some hold the potential to alienate working-class students from their middle-class peers. Instead, practitioners may want to explore ways to provide employment opportunities closely associated with academic majors and prospective careers.

Practitioners can also seek to provide paid involvement opportunities to support students' sense of belonging on campus, such as positions in student programming or activities boards, peer tutors, mentors, or cultural ambassadors. Schwartz et al. (2009)

indicated these opportunities can be linked to students' cultural identities and values, such as outreach efforts to their own communities (Ortiz, 2004). Resident assistant and other peer mentoring positions may help working-class students earn income and provide access to on-campus housing at no or reduced cost while promoting their social integration and leadership development. All of these opportunities can enhance working-class students' social, cultural, academic, and human capital.

Working-Class Students' Social Integration

Students' class background encourages or discourages their participation in organizations and extracurricular activities based on the types of social capital inherited from parents (Stuber, 2011). Students from more advantaged backgrounds arrive on campus with a good deal of social capital derived from pre-existing networks (e.g., sports leagues, camps, and private educational systems; Aries, 2008). They have also "internalized the intensive socialization of their parents … to engage independently in behaviors and activities that cultivate their social and cultural capital," whereas working-class students are more likely to be involved in activities primarily designed to enhance their eligibility for employment (Stuber, 2011, p. 70).

Working-class students are significantly less likely to belong to student groups, participate in extracurricular experiences, or serve in student organizational leadership positions than their middle- and upper-class peers (Rubin, 2012a, 2012b; Soria, Hussein, & Vue, 2014; Terenzini et al., 2001; Walpole, 2003). Walpole (2003) estimated that half of working-class students spend less than one hour a week in student organizations. They are also less likely to live on campus and participate in residence hall activities (Rubin, 2012b). While the decision to live at home frequently has an economic basis, it is negatively associated with students' extracurricular involvement, engagement in academic activities with peers, and ability to make friends on campus (Witkow, Gillen-O'Neel, & Fuligni, 2012). Because they may be commuting to campus and are likely employed at least part-time, working-class students are also less likely to spend time in nonacademic activities, such as sharing meals with friends, engaging in out-of-class conversations, and spending time with friends on campus (Armstrong & Hamilton, 2013; Rubin, 2012a, 2012b; Soria, 2013c). As a consequence of these differences, working-class students may be less likely to develop friendships with their peers—a factor that could compromise their social integration on campus (Pascarella & Terenzini, 2005; Tinto, 1993).

There are academic implications for working-class students' lower social integration. Relationships with other students provide access to informational support, such as assistance on assignments (Rubin, 2012b). Social integration is also a strong predictor of students' academic performance and retention (Robbins et al., 2004). According to Astin (1993), peers are "the single most potent source of influence," affecting virtually every aspect of students' growth, including their cognitive, affective, psychological, and behavioral development (p. 398). Consequently, working-class students who miss out on opportunities to become socially integrated on their campuses may also encounter challenges achieving academic success and development.

Barriers to Peer Interactions, Extracurricular Involvement, and Social Integration

Involvement on campus has a clear economic component. The costs of engagement are borne in many ways—through student fees, travel to and from campus, childcare arrangements, or missed time from work. Students from lower socioeconomic backgrounds often cannot afford the financial obligations of social activities or membership in Greek-letter organizations (Stuber, 2011; Walpole, 2011). Middle-class students are twice as likely as working-class students to participate in sororities and fraternities (Stuber, 2011). Similarly, using a multi-institutional data set from nine large public universities, Soria (2013b) found 11.4% of wealthy and 7.2% of upper-middle- and professional-class students lived in fraternity or sorority housing, compared to 1.5% of working-class students.

Campuses can mitigate the economic impact of involvement by implementing policies and practices to make cocurricular participation more affordable. For example, the student government association at Amherst College ensures all events it funds on campus are free to students (Aries, 2008), a policy working-class students perceived as an equalizing force. Practitioners should therefore work more actively to ensure that costs of engagement on campus are affordable (or non-existent) for working-class students.

Many working-class students feel a distinct sense of marginalization, isolation, and estrangement from their wealthier peers (Aries, 2008; Armstrong & Hamilton, 2013). Some of this may be attributed to a perceived insensitivity to issues regarding social class and finances (McLoughlin, 2012). The working-class students in McLoughlin's study reported several examples of cross-class friendships being challenged by the different levels of discretionary income between themselves and their peers, with the middle- and upper-class students often expecting working-class students to contribute as much as they did to meals or recreational pursuits. One working-class student in McLoughlin's study was pressured by a wealthier friend to join a sorority and, after expressing her inability to afford the dues, the friend suggested she simply get a second job to pay for the additional expense.

Sometimes, the challenges to cross-class peer relationships are much less benign. When fraternities and sororities hold White trash themed parties where students are encouraged to dress in wife beaters, work boots, and other redneck attire (McDaniels et al., 2014), working-class students see themselves, their families, and their communities mocked by some of the more elite, wealthier students on campus and are reminded of their low social status. The secondary socialization working-class students undergo in higher education therefore requires "ruthless subjugation to the customs" of the middle class (Matthys, 2013, p. 186) to either fit in or drop out. It is not surprising, then, that some working-class students in Matthys's study experienced a fear of the unknown and being rejected by others and, thus, decided not to pursue membership in these social organizations. Other research (Soria, 2013b) has found that working-class students who live in fraternities and sororities have a sense of belonging on par with middle- and upper-class students who are nonmembers, suggesting the potential for such involvement to enhance working-class students' sense of belonging in higher education in some cases.

Recommendations

Tinto (2012) noted that social affiliations are crucial because of the emotional support they provide to students—support that is expansive and leads to greater involvement in educational activities. Several researchers (Smith, 2007; Soria & Stebleton, 2013; Tierney & Venegas, 2006) have used theories of social capital to examine retention and persistence of college students. The working-class college students in Soria and Stebleton's (2013) study, for example, reported experiencing greater difficulty finding students in their classes with whom they could study, talking with faculty outside of class, identifying people on campus who shared their background and experiences, and locating a faculty or staff member to help them navigate their way through the university. In other words, they struggled to establish networks that might help them acquire social capital. Campuses can do a great deal to create the conditions—both within classrooms and outside them—where social networks might flourish. This section highlights a few possibilities.

First-generation students who participate in living-learning programs report a more successful academic and social transition to college than their first-generation peers who live in traditional residence hall settings (Inkelas, Daver, Vogt, & Leonard, 2007). Living-learning programs can also increase students' interactions with faculty, as most of the academic classes taught in a living-learning program are small. Furthermore, by increasing connections among students in the residence hall, participation in living-learning programs may help students from working-class backgrounds gain access to the social capital of their more affluent peers and become better connected to campus resources.

Peer mentorship and leadership programs can be embedded in many aspects of programmatic strategies to support working-class students in the transition to higher education. For example, peer mentors can serve as teaching assistants, tutors, academic coaches, and academic mentors in first-year seminars (Greenfield, Keup, & Gardner, 2013; Shook & Keup, 2012). They can also play key roles in precollege bridge programs, orientation, or residence life. Students are much more likely to go to peers than faculty or staff when they have questions or need support, but class differences can complicate the delivery of peer mentoring for working-class students. Peer leaders from working-class backgrounds can play an especially dynamic role in creating a safe space where similar students can share their concerns, develop a sense of community, and learn about campus traditions and expectations (Greenfield et al., 2013; Ward-Roof, 2010). Yet, students from working-class backgrounds do not participate in leadership roles as often as their peers from upper-income families (Soria, Hussein, et al., 2014); therefore, higher education practitioners should actively recruit working-class and first-generation students to peer leadership positions and remove potential barriers associated with participation (including lengthy commitments of time in workshops or trainings). Finally, all peer leaders should be trained to remain attentive to social-class differences so they can better identify the transition needs of students from working-class backgrounds (Espinoza, 2011).

Campus multicultural centers are particularly important in helping students connect with peers of similar and diverse cultural backgrounds (Patton, 2006); however, most multicultural centers do not include social class in their organizational frameworks. Instead, they tend to focus on affiliations based on racial, ethnic, religious, sexual orientation, and gender identity. U/Fused, or United for Undergraduate Socioeconomic Diversity, is a student-initiated movement with chapters on approximately 20 campuses across the United States. The purpose of U/Fused is to "increase socioeconomic diversity on campus, improve outcomes for low-income and working-class students, and foster dialogue on class issues" (Kahlenberg, 2013). Similar initiatives can be found at the University of Wisconsin (UW) at Madison (Schmidt, 2010) and the University of Chicago (Miller, 2013). The Working-Class Student Union at the UW–Madison offers peer counseling, peer advocates, social and educational events for first-generation, nontraditional transfer, and working-class students. The mission of the Union also extends to educating the campus about the benefits of celebrating social class diversity and, to that end, students involved in the Union provide educational workshops to student organizations, residence halls, students, and faculty. At the University of Chicago, the student organization Socioeconomic Acceptance and Diversity Alliance advocates for more resources for low-income students, creates a social venue welcoming to them, and aims to make social-class concerns more visible by holding campuswide discussions on class. The student organization recently developed a survey to learn more about the experiences of low-income students to share the results with campus administrators.

Institutions should continue to expand the availability of these social identity groups for the benefit of students from working-class backgrounds. This will be a challenging task because, as Lehmann (2007) noted, working-class students may not always identify their concerns as class-based. Therefore, educators who identify as working-class themselves are encouraged to initiate these groups with students and serve as organization advisors. Warnock (2014), a professor who worked at a small, private liberal arts college, described the successes and challenges of helping low-income, first-generation, and working-class students (LIFGWC) start a student organization. First, she connected with LIFGWC students after sharing her experiences as a low-income undergraduate on a campuswide panel. However, after gaining momentum to start an organization for LIFGWC students, Warnock and students found recruiting new members to be difficult, which they attributed to the fear and stigma associated with openly identifying as LIFGWC. In seeking ways to recruit LIFGWC students in a less public fashion, they encountered more roadblocks because the institution had no formal means of identifying these students other than to send an e-mail to students who received Pell grants. Warnock's experience speaks to the fact that working-class students are invisible within institutions, yet it also provides a silver lining of hope that faculty can intervene and help students develop social structures (e.g., student organizations) within which they can acquire camaraderie with peers from similar social-class backgrounds.

College students arrive on campus with their "coalition detection system engaged" (Tienda, 2013, p. 471), meaning they are aware of their differences and seek to join homogenous groups—processes that reinforce group boundaries. Institutions that merely bring students from diverse social, economic, ideological, and demographic backgrounds to their campuses reproduce existing group boundaries (Tienda, 2013); therefore, it is necessary to activate coalition-building systems that require students to have experiences on campus and interact with others in ways that challenge pre-existing group stereotypes (Crisp & Turner, 2011; Haring-Smith, 2012; Tienda, 2013). While class-based student organizations and activities can serve as a place of belonging and understanding for working-class students, practitioners are advised to move beyond this to engage in meaningful intergroup dialogues. In the absence of working-class student organizations, it is important that faculty and practitioners ensure that diverse social-class perspectives are included in cross-group interactions (Lehman, 2004).

Conclusion

Students from working-class backgrounds face challenges with regards to their social integration in higher education (Hurst, 2010; Stuber, 2011; Walpole, 2003). As a result, they may miss out on the many benefits of social integration—including enhanced development in self-esteem, cognitive, affective, and analytical skills (Astin, 1993). Working-class students who are not as involved on campus may also lack access to important social, cultural, academic, and human capital that can enhance their success after graduation (Stuber, 2011; Walpole, 2003). The consequences of lower social integration can run much deeper and have profound implications for working-class students' futures because students who do not experience social integration are less likely to persist and complete their college degrees (Pascarella & Terenzini, 2005; Tinto, 1993). In the concluding chapter, campuswide strategies to support working-class students in transition are addressed.

Chapter 6
STRATEGIES FOR CAMPUSWIDE REFORM TO SUPPORT WORKING-CLASS STUDENTS IN TRANSITION

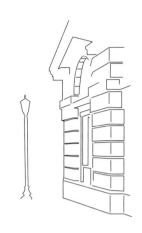

Academic capital formation theory is a framework for studying interventions that can encourage cross-generation educational attainment among students of color, low-income students, and first-generation college students (St. John et al., 2011; Winkle-Wagner, Bowman, & St. John, 2012). St. John et al. (2011) argued that four social processes engage students in overcoming barriers to higher education: (a) financial aid opportunities that ease family concerns about educational costs; (b) mentors, teachers, and community leaders who develop supportive social networks in schools and communities and help parents and students overcome fears about pursuing a higher education by transmitting knowledge about college; (c) mentors and social networks who help students navigate systems and barriers by building knowledge about how to handle classism and racism; and (d) accurate, trustworthy information received at critical moments.

Similarly, Espinoza's (2011) pivotal moment framework provides guidance on how to create the networks needed to support student success in college. Educators can create a lasting impact on students by engaging them in experiences, or pivotal moments, that transform "their social and psychological orientations toward academic achievement" (Espinoza, 2011, p. 4). Caring faculty and administrators can also help students acquire the knowledge and interpersonal skills needed for success in academia. Espinoza suggested that educators position themselves to create these pivotal moments by (a) understanding the obstacles students face; (b) intervening early through intrusive advising approaches; (c) involving parents and family; (d) helping students navigate the educational system by providing academic and social support; (e) offering comprehensive, long-term support; (f) encouraging systematic reforms; (g) making financial aid assistance available; and (h) training future educators who can also work effectively with disadvantaged students.

By alleviating cost concerns, enhancing networking opportunities, and facilitating trustworthy mentoring relationships that transmit cultural capital, institutions can help students develop learning habits that enable their academic progress and build social capital

(St. John et al., 2011). This understanding of academic capital formation and the pivotal moment framework guides the policies and strategies described in this chapter. In particular, the chapter examines institutional policies that determine access, strategies for building support networks for students and parents (both before college entry and after matriculation), and the ongoing need to make class visible on college and university campuses. While not exhaustive, these concluding recommendations suggest important first steps institutions might take to ensure working-class college students have access to and success in higher education, thus breaking patterns of social reproduction.

Institutional Policy Level

Elsewhere in this volume, the impact of admissions and financial aid policies on working-class students' access to and success in postsecondary education has been described. This section offers considerations for restructuring college admissions policies so they are more sensitive to class issues. It also addresses practical strategies for helping working-class students manage financial barriers to college success and completion.

Restructuring Admissions Policies

Several authors have suggested that colleges and universities restructure their admissions policies to allow all applicants to compete on more even terms, including removing legacy admissions policies and early-action on early-decision programs (Golden, 2006; Kahlenberg, 2010; Stevens, 2007). Legacy admissions for children of alumni have had deleterious effects for students of color and low-income students seeking admission at prestigious universities because the beneficiaries of such policies have historically been disproportionately White, Protestant, upper-class students (Lind, 2010). Although affirmative action policies are viewed contentiously in America, more White students have gained admission to top-tier institutions under legacy admissions than students of color have gained admission because of affirmative action policies, and, in some institutions, there are more White legacy students than students of color combined (Brittain & Bloom, 2010; Lind, 2010). Since legacy applicants are admitted at two to four times the rates of nonlegacy applicants (Golden, 2010), working-class students are likely to receive more equitable opportunities for admission if legacy policies are abolished.

Enrollment managers and admissions staff are encouraged to examine the impact of such policies on their efforts to increase diversity on campus. For example, Texas A&M University abolished its school legacy program after learning that the program overwhelmingly benefitted White students over students of color (Ackerman, 2004). It is difficult to sort out the effects of this policy shift, as Texas has since adopted the Top 10 Percent plan, which guarantees admission to high-performing high school graduates. These types of initiatives encourage geographic diversity and may open doors to some low-income or underrepresented minority students who may not have previously been competitive candidates because of the focus on test scores rather than high performance (Potter, 2014)—another admissions policy requiring evaluation.

Given some of the previously discussed concerns about standardized testing, colleges and universities are encouraged to evaluate multiple measures of students' abilities to be successful in higher education so as to better level the playing field for working-class college students (Fullinwider & Lichtenberg, 2004). Admissions evaluations should include a wider range of nonacademic experience (e.g., employment, caregiver responsibilities) as evidence of leadership and interpersonal development and of the maturity needed to succeed in college. It is also important to recognize that working-class students' employment experiences may not be prestigious (e.g., an internship at a law firm), reflecting instead the availability of opportunities in their immediate neighborhoods (e.g., grocery store clerk). As such, admissions evaluators should take regional, economic, and community contexts into consideration when evaluating students' employment experiences.

Finally, as noted elsewhere in this volume, participation in early-action and early-decision programs can have negative implications for working-class students, especially with respect to financing college. While admissions professionals may agree in theory that these policies are problematic for some students, they are unlikely to drop them if they feel this puts them at a competitive disadvantage with respect to peer institutions. As such, the elimination of early-action or early-decision programs may require collective action on the part of a number of institutions if no one is willing to be first. Further, as Fullinwider and Lichtenberg (2004) made clear, no college would be seriously disadvantaged if such programs were collectively abolished by a group of peer institutions. Where wholesale policy change seems unlikely, higher education practitioners can take steps to inform working-class students about the potential negative effects of early-action and early-decision programs by partnering with precollege programs or high school guidance counselors. Intentional partnerships with high schools in working-class neighborhoods or precollege programs, such as College Possible (2013), can make it much easier to promote the availability of early-action or early-decision programs to students who can benefit from such information. For instance, College Possible provides comprehensive support to low-income junior and senior high school students by enrolling them in 320 hours of after-school curriculum focused on preparing for entrance exams and completing college and financial aid applications. The high school students are coached through their transition to higher education and receive support all the way through college graduation. The college curriculum for students includes improving study skills, building time management skills, connecting with campus, choosing a major, tackling family demands, and financial planning, among other areas.

Financial Considerations

Researchers have advocated several strategies to increase the access to and affordability of higher education for working-class students. One step to achieve these outcomes is to provide more information about financial aid opportunities and the true cost of attendance for students from low-income backgrounds. Studies suggest working-class students and their families are poorly informed about financial aid opportunities (Horn, Chen, & Chapman, 2003). Many college students do not submit financial aid applications (including the Free Application for Federal Student Aid, or FAFSA) and, thus, never learn whether they may be eligible for financial aid. For example, in the 2007-2008 school year, a total of 8.4 million college students—representing 40.9% of all students nationwide—did not apply for financial aid (Kantrowitz, 2009). Of those, an estimated 2.3 million students would likely have had an expected family contribution that would have made them eligible for a federal Pell Grant; 1.1 million potentially would have been qualified for a *full* Pell Grant (Kantrowitz, 2009). Although financial aid application rates increase each year, King (2006) discovered that students in the lowest-income brackets were *less likely* to have submitted financial applications in a five-year time frame (between 1999-2000 and 2003-2004), and that more than half the students who applied for financial aid did not meet important deadlines that may have made them eligible for additional state grants. The majority of students who do not apply for financial aid believe they are ineligible, do not want to take on debt, or do not have enough information about applying for financial aid (National Center for Education Statistics, 2008).

Perna, Lundy-Wagner, Yee, Brill, and Tadal (2011) lauded higher education institutions for providing more generous institutional aid packages to eliminate financial barriers for working-class students; however, they also critiqued these institutions for remaining "bastions of privilege" by failing to adequately communicate information about this aid to prospective students" (p. 89). The authors recommended providing clear and visible information about financial aid in several locations on university websites, hiring additional financial aid staff to conduct outreach to working-class families with respect to the financial aid process, and visiting high schools to share information with students. Partnerships with precollege outreach and transition programs can also be effective, and practitioners should reach out to these programs rather than relying on the programs to connect with them. Because working-class students may be more likely to enroll close to home, partnerships with local K-12 school districts and community colleges may be especially beneficial.

Institutions can also rethink the ways in which aid eligibility is determined and place more emphasis on providing need-based aid, as middle- and upper-income students are more likely than working-class students to benefit from merit-based financial support (Dynarski, 2004; Rubenstein & Scafidi, 2002). Through their research of low-income students, St. John et al. (2011) acknowledged the importance of finances in framing the students' and their parents' expectations of higher education attendance. Yet, they also discovered that low-income and first-generation students who received guaranteed financial aid through the Indiana Twenty-First Century Scholars and Washington State Achievers programs were much more likely to complete advanced courses during high school. St. John et al. stressed that the guaranteed, trustworthy forms of financial aid eased cost concerns and allowed students to develop "strong internal images of themselves as college students and become active in pursuing their educational goals within their high schools" (p. 109). Students' parents also became advocates for access to high-quality courses after learning their children would receive guaranteed financial aid to attend college.

Working-class students who do receive financial assistance may find that it is inadequate to cover all the costs associated with college attendance, such as living on campus, participating in cocurricular activities, or purchasing supplies for coursework. If working-class students cannot afford to travel home during breaks, they may scramble to secure housing or incur extra fees for remaining on campus when residence halls are closed (Kezar, 2011). Meal plans are an additional financial burden that may be required on some campuses or for some groups (e.g., first-year students, those living in a particular residence hall). Students from lower SES backgrounds may be more likely than their peers to work to pay for these expenses, but Soria, Weiner, et al. (2014) and Armstrong and Hamilton (2013) also discovered working-class students were significantly more likely to skip meals to afford college than their middle- and upper-class peers. Given the benefits of living on campus and the necessity of food security, colleges and universities should take more active steps to lower the costs of housing and meal plans for students with the greatest financial need. Sliding scales based on family income, alternative residence halls for students who need to live on campus during breaks, scholarships for living on campus, or discounted room and board costs can better support working-class students who wish to live on campus.

Campuses can also take strides to examine ways in which some college expenses can be eliminated or reduced. For example, the University of Wisconsin at River Falls (2014) created a textbook rental program for all students, with rental fees embedded in tuition. Full-time students pay approximately $70 for textbook rental (part-time students pay a reduced rate), easily saving hundreds of dollars per semester. University technology programs can also help level the playing field for students who have less access to personal computing devices, such as laptops, tablets, and smartphones. Through a grant program, the College of Education and Human Development at the University of Minnesota, Twin Cities provided all incoming first-year students with free iPads (Wagoner, Schwalbe, Hoover, & Ernst, 2012). Twenty-seven instructors teaching the college's first-year seminar incorporated the tablets into their curricula, with a significant number of both instructors and students believing that the iPads encouraged active and experiential learning that supported students' knowledge acquisition. Similarly, Ursinus College (2014) provides free laptop computers to all incoming students so that "regardless of financial need, no one is left behind" (para. 5).

Developing Precollege Support Networks

As noted in the previous chapters, student involvement and sense of belonging on campus has significant implications for satisfaction, persistence, and academic success. Yet, many working-class students who are successful in higher education attribute much of their success to finding a mentor in high school who provided the hope and confidence they needed to pursue an undergraduate degree (Beegle, 2009). Espinoza (2011) suggested mentors can serve as advisors, advocates, and supporters to help working-class students navigate a variety of transitions. Beegle (2009) emphasized the importance of mentorship, noting that people who move out of poverty rarely attribute their success to a program; instead, they describe individuals who cared about them and went above and beyond to tell them they were special, helped them gain confidence, did not judge them based on their economic circumstances, believed there was a way out of poverty, ensured access to resources to meet basic needs and overcome roadblocks, and connected them to others who could support their educational journeys. In short, effective mentors share their social and cultural capital with their protégés.

Unfortunately working-class students are less likely to receive encouragement from counselors, teachers, and parents to participate in postsecondary education and are, therefore, also less likely to possess knowledge about higher education or have access to networks that could transmit college-going knowledge. High student–counselor ratios and time constraints limit working-class students' access to such knowledge. A single counselor may serve 471 students and is likely to spend 38 minutes on average discussing college admission with a student (Keaton, 2012; McDonough, 2005). College prospects from upper-income families increasingly pay for counseling services or enroll at better resourced high schools with lower counselor-to-student ratios, further distinguishing middle- and upper-class students from their working-class peers with regards to their preparation for college (Golden, 2006; Stevens, 2007).

As such, working-class students stand to benefit greatly from formal educational partnerships among colleges, middle schools, and high schools. While college admissions staff are the campus employees most likely to conduct outreach efforts to high schools, academic advisors are also encouraged to visit local schools to work individually with students. They can work proactively to provide more information regarding college entrance exams and financial aid applications to working-class high school students (Hurst, 2012). The current culture of academic advising suggests that many advisors expect students to navigate the complex university environment to visit them in their offices; however, working-class students would be better supported if advisors left their offices to engage students in their own communities. In my own professional work as college academic advisor at the University of Alaska Anchorage, I worked one-on-one with low-income students within high school guidance counseling offices to help them register for college entrance exams, complete their financial aid applications, apply for admission to the university, and select and register for classes online once they were admitted. Soria and Bultmann (2014) suggested that academic advisors are instrumental sources of support for working-class students because they offer students social, academic, and cultural capital they may not be able to acquire elsewhere.

Several existing federal grant programs can also provide systems of support and transmit social, academic, and cultural capital for working-class students. For example, the TRIO programs Educational Talent Search and Upward Bound provide tutoring, academic support, financial aid workshops, academic skills development, and mentorship to first-generation and low-income middle and high school students. Furthermore, TRIO programs help students overcome social and cultural barriers to higher education (Graham, 2011), fostering greater educational aspirations and a better understanding of academic resources (Child, 1998; Myers & Shirm, 1999). TRIO participants are also more likely to complete their bachelor's degrees and continue to graduate school than are their peers (Balz & Esten, 1998).

Despite the successes of TRIO programs in preparing high school students for college, a critical shortage of funding limits the availability of such programs for low-income and first-generation students who need access. It is estimated that only 5% of all students eligible for TRIO programs can be served (Balz & Esten, 1998), and recent governmental budget cuts further limit access to TRIO for eligible students. To address those disparities, colleges and universities can create TRIO-like educational programs on their campuses. For example, in addition to comprehensive aid packages designed to reduce the financial burden of attendance (including guarantees that students will not have to incur debt to attend), some universities offer financial aid counseling, faculty mentorship, and laptops to low-income students (Pallais & Turner, 2007). The University of Nebraska has formed intensive college preparatory programs for first-generation students featuring counseling, tutoring, peer mentorship, summer courses, and science camps within local high schools (Chau, 2012). If participating high school students continually meet grade point average requirements, the University has guaranteed to meet any outstanding financial need not covered by grants and scholarships so that they can avoid incurring student loan debt.

Parental Support Networks

Scholars have demonstrated the importance of parental involvement and support in predicting college student outcomes including academic achievement, educational aspirations, adjustment to higher education, development of college student identity, and commitment to graduation (Bryan & Simmons, 2009; Dennis, Phinney, & Chuateco, 2005; Fullinwider & Lichtenberg, 2004). Yet, working-class students, who are often the first in their families to attend college, may have limited access to knowledgeable support and guidance from their parents as they transition to higher education. Therefore, college and university practitioners are encouraged to work closely with parents of working-class students to provide them with information about higher education long before students apply. Parents who are well informed about colleges and universities are more likely to envision their children as college students, become strong advocates in helping them gain access to advanced courses in high school, and be engaged in the transitions their children will face (St. John et al., 2011). It is challenging for working-class parents to advocate for their children in educational systems within which they have no experience; therefore, it is critical that college and university practitioners intentionally reach out to provide assistance rather than expecting parents to ask for help themselves. Parents are more likely to be engaged in helping their children select colleges, choose majors, and prepare for the transition to higher education if there is a bond of trust between parents and college support personnel (St. John et al., 2011).

Yet first-generation students face many challenges integrating their academic and family lives, and college practitioners can be instrumental in preparing parents for some of the challenges they may encounter when their children enroll in college. For example, Bryan and Simmons (2009) found that first-generation students were not that interested in sharing their campus lives with their parents and, in turn, the parents did not spend extended periods of time visiting their children on campus. The authors hypothesized first-generation students kept their family and college lives separate for several reasons; namely, their parents did not demonstrate much interest in their academic lives, were intimidated by the college setting, and did not understand their experiences on campus, leading to a sense of frustration when it came to communicating educational plans.

Similarly, Aries (2008) found that first-generation students who lived on campus some distance from their homes did not see their family members much during the year because they could not afford trips back home. At the same time, working-class parents may not be able to afford to take time away from work or may lack the flexibility in their work schedules to travel and visit their children. Some students avoided family visits to campus because they did not want their parents to feel uncomfortable. First-generation students also felt pressure from their parents, whom they perceived were living vicariously through them —a pressure that was burdensome because students felt obligated to do the things their parents could not do in college. As a result, many working-class students perceive real and symbolic distances between themselves and their parents. Structured opportunities for greater family involvement may help working-class students integrate their family backgrounds into their college life which can, in turn, help students achieve a stronger sense of fit with their institutions (Covarrubias, Romero, & Trivelli, 2014). Family weekends featuring free or heavily discounted lodging and transportation can make it easier for working-class parents to participate. Even bring-your-parents-to-class days may help *all* parents—not just those from working-class families—better connect with their children's academic experiences in college. Online newsletters, parent portals, and web conferences are possible strategies for engaging parents and family members who cannot take part in campus-based events.

College and university practitioners can also work beyond individual families and reach into communities by partnering with key community leaders and advocates. Supportive adults outside of families who are also considered to be trustworthy sources of information (e.g., teachers, mentors, college staff, and community leaders) are significant in helping working-class students navigate pathways in and through higher education (Soria & Stebleton, 2013; Stanton-Salazar, 1997). Many working-class students suggested that information from these individuals mattered more than printed guidebooks, details on college costs, or other official information (St. John et al., 2011). Students tended to filter information through their trusted sources, observations, and inner experiences or reactions to critical situations when making major decisions in college. Individual relationships are thus key in helping working-class students make successful transitions to higher education.

Programmatic Practices of Inclusion

Institutions are encouraged to actively examine their existing structures and develop new ones that will create a more welcoming environment for working-class students, who may not be as likely to ask questions about higher education processes for fear that doing so will make them feel like outsiders or expose them as not belonging (Kezar, 2011). Orientation and transition programs can encourage student interactions, promote academic and social integration, and make the hidden rules of higher education more visible to working-class students (Borrego, 2008; Kezar, 2011; Soria, Lingren Clark, & Koch, 2013). Despite these benefits, orientation may also be a financial hardship for some students. Charging a fee for orientation and requiring attendance in lengthier (e.g., full week-long) programs (Soria et al., 2013) may be challenging for working-class students, leading them to opt out or feel burdened by the extra expenses and time away from family or employment. Orientation programs that feature expense-free programming—including meals, transportation options, and childcare—in addition to stipends for attendance may reduce barriers for working-class students.

Other than financial aid, bridge programs represent the most common institutional practices to support historically underrepresented student groups transitioning to higher education (Greenfield et al., 2013). Bridge programs can help working-class first-year students experience a welcoming campus climate before classes begin and further enhance their sense of belonging through the early development of faculty and peer relationships. To some extent, the friendships and connections working-class students develop in precollege bridge programs can parallel those social networks middle- and upper-class students often bring to campus (Aries, 2008). Within larger institutions, bridge programs connect working-class students with advisors and faculty who can serve as supporters, cultural brokers, and mentors; connect students with prospective employment and engagement opportunities on campus; and orient students to campus life. Working-class students who participate in such programs are better positioned to develop self-confidence, become integrated and connected to the campus community, have meaningful interactions with faculty in small class settings, and build stronger academic skills (Greenfield et al., 2013; Kezar, 2000; Terenzini et al., 1996).

Precollege bridge programs do not have to require lengthy on-campus stays to achieve these outcomes. The first-generation students in Bryan and Simmons's (2009) study believed they benefitted from making several short on-campus college visits before formally enrolling. The students participated in workshops within an early intervention program that helped them feel more comfortable on campus and eased the stress of the impending move to college for both them and their parents.

Because bridge programs are a popular intervention strategy for at-risk populations, students may feel deficient in their academic skills or ability to succeed in college. To combat these negative perceptions, the focus of such programs should be on building the existing strengths of students and developing a community of learners who share common narratives and experiences while avoiding the impression that they possess fewer inherent skills or abilities to be successful than other college students (Martinez, Sher, Krull, & Wood, 2009). Inviting working-class students to share how they feel they can best be supported in their transition as opposed to making assumptions about what they need can also alleviate their feelings of deficiency.

Working-class students' initial encounters with front-line personnel (e.g., financial aid services, admissions offices, career services, academic advising offices) have a significant impact on the extent to which they perceive the institution as welcoming. Martinez and colleagues (2009) recommended practitioners avoid showing surprise or disdain toward those who do not appear to know college procedures commonly known to middle-class students. Practitioners should instead approach students without assumptions about their level of college knowledge and offer guidance in a neutral manner. Front-line service staff, who, on many college campuses, also include student employees, should also be trained to better understand the precollege experiences of first-generation and working-class students and to give full, complete information to students, rather than expecting them to know campus jargon, acronyms, or idiosyncrasies.

Many working-class students possess a great deal of pride in the values they learned growing up in working-class families, including having a strong work ethic and the discipline needed to complete work-related tasks (Aries, 2008; Hurst, 2010; Stuber, 2011). Those students often identified with the work ethics of their parents and believed that hard work was the basis of their accomplishments. They often perceived themselves as more hard working, self-reliant, mature, responsible, and independent than peers from middle- and upper-class backgrounds (Aries, 2008; Lehmann, 2009). Upwardly mobile working-class students who attend universities often cope by drawing upon attributes such as determination, self-reliance, and the ability to cope with adversity (Reay, Crozier, & Clayton, 2009). These values can support working-class students as they make transitions to higher education, yet because working-class college students are likely to be employed while enrolled, they may feel as though they are better able to apply their work ethic and discipline in the familiar world of employment than that of academics. Therefore, advisors and faculty seeking to support working-class students who may be struggling in academic areas may wish to advise students to apply their work ethic to academic work by envisioning college as a job to be prioritized and completed even in the midst of other responsibilities.

Drawing on strengths-based advising practices, academic advisors and other student affairs practitioners can help working-class students acculturate to the new social and cultural norms of campus while still maintaining and valuing their social class identities. Strengths-based advising practices are promising ways in which academic advisors can work to enhance the esteem of working-class students who are transitioning to higher education. Founded on the principles of positive psychology, strengths-based approaches involve the identification, development, and utilization of individuals' top talents in order to encourage growth and personal achievement (Hodges & Clifton, 2004). Rather than assessing students' deficiencies, advisors using strengths-based approaches explore the personal talents students bring into college and help them leverage those talents to address challenges, obstacles, or opportunities (Schreiner, 2013). Strengths-based interventions actively promote college student engagement and retention through the premise that students who identify and apply their strengths will be more focused on their academic and career goals (Soria & Stubblefield, 2014). These perspectives can be especially useful in promoting first-year students' academic self-efficacy, retention, and sense of belonging on campus (Soria & Stubblefield, in press). Academic advisors can help working-class students apply their strengths in the process of learning, intellectual development, and academic achievement to increase their desired levels of productivity and personal excellence.

TRIO programs can also provide continued vital social support networks for working-class students as they transition into graduate education. For example, undergraduate students conducting research through the Ronald E. McNair Program benefit from enhanced academic and social integration in graduate school, a greater sense of competence in the knowledge and skills necessary to be successful in advanced study, and better understanding of graduate-level expectations (Gittens, 2014). McNair scholars also reported receiving many opportunities to network with others to create new learning communities (Gittens, 2014). Policymakers and institutional leaders should work in tandem to back these programs and connect incoming students to these institutional support structures.

The journey to higher educational attainment for working-class students necessarily involves a "motivation to remain on the path that must be generated from within" (Lucey et al., 2003, p. 297); therefore, while institutions can develop programmatic strategies to assist working-class students in transition, they must attend to internal matters as well. The shifts that working-class students make out of their social-class spheres sometimes require internal and external changes involving the pain of separation and a loss of identity (Reay, 1997). Lippincott and German (2007) offered suggestions for college counselors to help working-class students navigate these difficult transitions, including reassuring students that they are deserving and capable of achieving a college education (Stephens, Fryberg, Markus, Johnson, & Covarrubias, 2012) and engaging them in group counseling opportunities with other first-generation students.

Many, but not all, working-class students are also the first in their families to attend college. While psychological support and counseling services designed specifically for working-class students may help them navigate the liminal spaces they inhabit due to their tenuous position in two different social classes, programmatic opportunities designed for first-generation students may also provide opportunities to develop their voice and experience validation. Class Action (2014) hosts three-day, first-in-the-family digital storytelling projects on campuses to help first-generation college students craft first-person narratives examining their own educational success and develop counter-narratives to the deficit language typically used to describe them. Colleges and universities can also collaborate with existing media programs on campus to help first-generation students develop voice and place within the institution.

Creating Inclusive Campuses and Making Class Visible

On campuses, classism is negatively associated with several dimensions of college students' experiences, including their sense of belonging, academic adjustment, and social adjustment (Ostrove, 2007). At the same time, policy leaders continue to call for higher education institutions to open access to students from diverse backgrounds and to ensure the success of these diverse students. As such, they cannot ignore the existence of classism within postsecondary education. Rather, policy leaders should provide support to infuse higher education structures with a deeper understanding of multicultural awareness that includes social class. It is not enough for institutions simply to provide more financial aid to increase affordability for lower SES students; instead, senior administrators (e.g., presidents, chancellors, vice presidents, provosts, deans) who have the power and resources to set campus climate agendas (Banks, 2009; Hale, 2004) must be inclusive of class concerns just as they include other forms of oppression.

Social class affects psychological factors (e.g., decision making, self-perception, agency, attitudes) and everyday interpersonal interactions (e.g., employment relationships, parenting styles, linguistics, social status; Fiske & Markus, 2012). As such, efforts to disrupt an individual's thoughts about and relationship to class can be quite challenging. Faculty and staff development programs should seek to increase employees' understanding of class differences (Vander Putten, 2001) in addition to competency with other more traditionally recognized forms of diversity. Beegle (2009) provided several guidelines to help practitioners and organizations move toward effecting greater change and disrupting patterns of intergenerational poverty, with cultural competency serving as the bedrock for organizational change. To build those competencies, staff and faculty can learn more about some of the unspoken rules of social class and how they may affect students' perceptions of the higher education system; recognize when their own teaching or advising styles may be incongruent with the class-based learning preferences of students, and engage in critical self-awareness of their own class-based ways of understanding (Payne, 2005). Knowledge of class structures must extend beyond the limited sphere of economics into the cultural, symbolic, and social aspects associated with social classes. As faculty and staff gain more knowledge, it remains important that they continue to check their assumptions about students from different social-class backgrounds.

Many staff and faculty receive few opportunities to engage in professional development opportunities, including diversity awareness and appreciation (Banks, 2009). All campus employees—including those who work in residential life, bookstores, food services, counseling settings, safety and security—should receive opportunities to engage in consistent training situated in critical theoretical knowledge about how to negotiate social class differences. Such training can alleviate cultural tensions and help staff act as allies for working-class students (Banks, 2009).

Banks (2009) recommended that faculty, administrators, and staff critically analyze their relationships with issues of class, race, and gender and engage in narrative work around their positions in social locations and how those positions shape their views, their reactions to students with whom they come in contact, and how they have been socialized to develop their deeply held beliefs about students from different backgrounds. This essential work can occur through formal and informal discussions about social class. Common book readings around openly critical and engaging work—such as *Nickel and Dimed: On (Not) Getting by In America* (Ehrenreich, 2001), an autobiography of a woman who went "undercover" and worked in a series of low-wage positions for one year, or *Class Matters* (*The New York Times,* 2005), a series by a team of reporters about social class in America—could be the basis for such discussions. While those texts address larger social-class issues in the United States, Hurst (2010, 2012), Aries (2008), and Stuber (2011) present first-hand accounts of working-class students enrolled in colleges and universities, which may be more essential readings for practitioners seeking to understand these students' experiences in higher education.

Working-class students may internalize their struggles because social class is invisible on college campuses—few campus resources, courses, or student programs currently address social-class issues. The challenge, therefore, is to make class visible, which can happen in many ways. First, administrators can more actively identify the class origins of students, faculty, and staff and also make these data public on any documentation or websites highlighting campus diversity (Oldfield, 2012). Jonas (1999) acknowledged that the reluctance to create a social-class index in the United States is rooted in political reasons: Formally measuring class would force U.S. politicians and policymakers to acknowledge social-class divisions exist. If colleges and universities list no social-class data on their websites, then it goes without saying that they also fail to publicize retention and graduation rates of students or hiring and promotion rates of faculty and staff from different social-class backgrounds. The absence of data points addressing those areas reifies upper-class hegemony, undermines the importance of social class, and, ultimately, sweeps class-based inequalities under the rug. Without those data, it is nearly impossible for campus administrators to understand how well they are serving working-class students, if they are achieving diversity or social justice missions, and whether they are continuing class-based discriminatory practices in hiring and promotion. Although it is not necessarily easy to define social class, the British government has achieved success (Oldfield, 2012) by incorporating a well-known sociological classification (i.e., the Goldthorpe Schema, see Goldthorpe, 2007) as the basis for their National Statistics Socioeconomic Classification (Office for National Statistics, 2010). This system of classification is highly occupation based, and it would be easy for higher education institutions in the United States to obtain similar data from their students through self-reports at the point of admission (Rubin et al., 2014; Soria & Barratt, 2012) or by calculating a composite social-class score based on parents' education, family income, Pell grant status, or other measures.

It is also important to help middle- and upper-class college students recognize their own privilege and prejudices against lower social classes to heighten awareness and inspire social change among these dominant cultural groups (Mayhew & Fernandez, 2007; Schwartz et al., 2009). Among other themes of diversity in campus organizations and student programming, themes related to social class issues should be present. At Dartmouth College (2013), for example, Class Divide, a three-year cross-campus and community programming initiative, featured a series of events and performances to raise awareness and spark conversations about social class. Community sharing circles told stories of social-class division, the president of the university was interviewed about his own upbringing in a rural mining community, students were invited to mail in postcards anonymously with their social-class secrets, and interviews were saved as podcasts available on their website. Such efforts highlight the ways in which social-class initiatives on campus can also be interdisciplinary in nature by inviting in the arts and community.

Gender and race are the primary factors given attention in the context of recruitment, affirmative action, and equality; however, dismissing class as an important mediator of educational, occupational, and economic outcomes perpetuates class-based inequalities. To illustrate this point, Vander Putten (2001) offered that considerations of only race and gender would functionally equate the experiences of Condoleeza Rice with those of an African American female housekeeper working at a hotel. Clearly, gender and race alone insufficiently address these women's unique experiences, abilities to navigate educational systems, and opportunities for social advancement. Without social-class identifiers in affirmative action policies, those from higher social-class backgrounds are more likely to enter positions of leadership and power due to their familiarity with these upper echelons. As such, Oldfield (2012) argued, "the current merit system is a class-based affirmative program that heavily favors those born of more fortunate circumstances" (p. 10). While Oldfield (2012) pressed campus administrators to ensure that its managerial ranks better reflect the nation's social-class diversity, that invitation can be extended to administrators as they consider the composition of the staff, faculty, and student body.

Additionally, practitioners and educators can conduct audits of their programs and curricula to ensure that content reflects the experiences of students from a variety of social-class backgrounds (Langhout, et al., 2009). Student affairs practitioners are encouraged to engage in dialogue with one another about the meaning of social class and how social-class identity intersects with college students' racial, ethnic, gender, and cultural identities (Borrego, 2004; Schwartz et al., 2009).

Consideration of race and gender on campus has increased appreciation of the contributions women and students of color bring to campus communities, equalized educational opportunities, and raised the collective consciousness about valuing these students (Vander Putten, 2001). When we "invite social class to the diversity table," similar outcomes can occur for working-class students (Vander Putten, 2001, p. 18). Organizational efforts to combat classism and support the needs of working-class students should be holistic in nature—it is not possible to transform institutional cultures in isolated siloes. Instead, collaborations between individuals with multiple voices and perspectives—including working-class students themselves—are necessary to achieve success in leveling the playing field for this population of students.

Conclusion

Higher education administrators, educators, and practitioners are encouraged to acknowledge the complex role that social class plays in students' lived experiences on campus. Recent studies of low-income and working-class students are leading practitioners, scholars, and administrators to develop new insights into the challenges facing them (Barratt, 2011; Kezar, 2011; Martin, 2012; Stuber, 2011; Walpole, 2007); however, issues of social class remain silent at many colleges and universities. Yet, it is a dimension of diversity that should not be overlooked when assessing the campus climate for underrepresented students. Furthermore, practitioners should consider the important role that they play in facilitating college students' sense of belonging and be more attuned to the frequency of their interactions with students from lower social-class backgrounds. Social class should continue to be brought to the forefront of discussions concerned with enhancing college students' success, social integration, and retention.

References

Abrahams, J., & Ingram, N. (2013). The chameleon habitus: Exploring local students' negotiations of multiple fields. *Sociological Research Online, 18*(4).

Ackerman, T. (2004, January 10). Texas A&M abolishes legacy program. *Houston Chronicle.* Retrieved from http://www.chron.com/news/houston-texas/article/Texas-A-M-abolishes-legacy-program-1959293.php

ACT and Council for Opportunity in Education. (2013). *The condition of college and career readiness 2013: First-generation students.* Retrieved from www.act.org/readiness/2013

Adelman, C. (1995). *The new college course map and transcript files: Changes in course-taking and achievement, 1972-1993.* Washington, DC: U.S. Department of Education.

Adelman, C. (2003). *Answers in the tool box: Academic intensity, attendance patterns, and bachelor's degree attainment.* Washington, DC: U.S. Department of Education.

Adelman, C. (2005). *Moving into town—and moving on: The community college in the lives of traditional-age students.* Washington, DC: U.S. Department of Education.

Adelman, C. (2006). *The toolbox revisited: Paths to degree completion from high school through college.* Washington, DC: U.S. Department of Education.

Advisory Committee on Student Financial Assistance. (2001). *Access denied: Restoring the nation's commitment to equal educational opportunity.* Washington, DC: Author.

Alvarez, L., & Kolker, A. (Producer). (2001). *People like us: Social class in America* [Film]. Washington, DC: Center for New American Media & WETA.

Archer, L., Pratt, S. D., & Phillips, D. (2001). Working-class men's constructions of masculinity and negotiations of (non)participation in higher education. *Gender and Education, 13*(4), 431-449.

Aries, E. (2008). *Race and class matters at an elite college.* Philadelphia, PA: Temple University Press.

Aries, E., & Seider, M. (2005). The interactive relationship between class identity and the college experience: The case of lower income students. *Qualitative Sociology, 28*(4), 419-443.

Armstrong, E. A., & Hamilton, L. T. (2013). *Paying for the party: How college maintains inequality.* Cambridge, MA: Harvard University Press.

Astin, A. W. (1993). *What happens in college? Four critical years revisited.* San Francisco, CA: Jossey-Bass.

Astin, A. W., & Oseguera, L. (2004). The declining "equity" of American higher education. *Review of Higher Education, 27*(3), 321-341.

Balz, F., & Esten, J. (1998). Fulfilling private dreams, serving public priorities: An analysis of TRIO students' success at independent colleges and universities. *Journal of Negro Education, 67*(4), 333-345.

Banks, C. (2009). *Black women undergraduates, cultural capital, and college success.* New York, NY: Peter Lang.

Barratt, W. (2007, April 25). Talking about social class on campus. *NASPA's Net Results.*

Barratt, W. (2011). *Social class on campus: Theories and manifestations.* Sterling, VA: Stylus Publishing.

Baxter, A., & Britton, C. (2001). Risk, identity, and change: Becoming a mature student. *International Studies in Sociology of Education, 11,* 87-102.

Beegle, D. M. (2009). *See poverty ... be the difference! Discover the missing pieces for helping people to move out of poverty.* Tigard, OR: Communication Across Barriers.

Berger, J. B. (2000). Optimizing capital, social reproduction, and undergraduate persistence: A sociological perspective. In J. M. Braxton (Ed.), *Reworking the student departure puzzle* (pp. 95-124). Nashville, TN: Vanderbilt University Press.

Bettie, J. (2000). Women without class: Chicas, Cholas, trash, and the presence/absence of class identity. *Signs: Journal of Women in Culture and Society, 26,* 1-35.

Block, P. (2008). *Community: The structure of belonging.* San Francisco, CA: Berrett-Koehler.

Borrego, S. E. (2004). *Class matters: Beyond access to inclusion.* Washington, DC: NASPA.

Borrego, S. E. (2008). Class on campus: Breaking the silence around socioeconomics. *Diversity & Democracy, 11,* 1-3.

Bourdieu, P. (1971). Intellectual field and creative project (S. France, Trans.). In M. F. D. Young (Ed.), *Knowledge and control: New directions for the sociology of education* (4th ed., pp. 161-188). London, England: Macmillan.

Bourdieu, P. (1984). *Distinction.* (R. Nice, Trans.). Cambridge, England: Polity.

Bourdieu, P. (1986). The forms of capital. In J. Richardson (Ed.), *Handbook of theory and research for the sociology of education* (pp. 241-258). Westport, CT: Greenwood Press.

Bourdieu, P. (1988). *Homo academicus.* (P. Collier, Trans.). Cambridge, England: Polity.

Bourdieu, P. (1996). *The state nobility: Elite schools in the field of power.* (L. C. Clough, Trans.). Cambridge, England: Polity.

Bourdieu, P. (1997). The forms of capital. In A. H. Halsey, H. Lauder, P. Brown, & A. S. Wells (Eds.), *Education: Culture, economy, and society* (pp. 46-58). Oxford, England: Oxford University Press.

Bourdieu, P. (2005). *The social structures of the economy.* Cambridge, England: Polity.

Bourdieu, P., & Passeron, J.-C. (1977). *Reproduction in education, society, and culture.* (R. Nice, Trans.). London, England: Sage.

Bourdieu, P., & Passeron, J.-C. (1979). *The inheritors, French students and their relation to culture.* (R. Nice, Trans.). Chicago, IL: University of Chicago Press.

Bourdieu, P., & Wacquant, L. J. D. (1992). *An invitation to reflexive sociology.* Chicago, IL: University of Chicago Press.

Bowen, W. G., Chingos, M. M., & McPherson, M. S. (2009). *Crossing the finish line: Completing college at America's public universities.* Princeton, NJ: Princeton University Press.

Bowen, W. G., Kurzweil, M. A., & Tobin, E. M. (2005). *Equity and excellence in American higher education.* Charlottesville, VA: University of Virginia Press.

Bowles, S., Gintis, H., & Groves, M. O. (2005). *Unequal chances: Family background and economic success.* New York, NY: Russell Sage Foundation.

Brantlinger, E. A. (2003). *Dividing classes: How the middle class negotiates and rationalizes school advantage.* New York, NY: RoutledgeFalmer.

Brittain, J., & Bloom, E. L. (2010). Admitting the truth: The effect of affirmative action, legacy preferences, and the meritocratic ideal on students of color in college admissions. In R. D. Kahlenberg (Ed.), *Affirmative action for the rich: Legacy preferences in college admissions* (pp. 123-142). New York, NY: The Century Foundation Press.

Bryan, E., & Simmons, L. A. (2009). Family involvement: Impacts on postsecondary educational success for first-generation Appalachian college students. *Journal of College Student Development, 50*(4), 391-406.

Calarco, J. M. (2014). Coached for the classroom: Parents' cultural transmission and children's reproduction of educational inequalities. *American Sociological Review.* Advanced online publication. doi:10.1177/0003122414546931

Callan, P. M. (2011). Reframing access and opportunity: Public policy dimensions. In D. E. Heller (Ed.), *The states and public higher education policy: Affordability, access, and accountability* (2nd ed., pp. 87-105). Baltimore, MD: The Johns Hopkins University Press.

Carnevale, A. P., & Desrochers, D. M. (2003). *Standards for what? The economic roots of K-16 reform.* Princeton, NJ: Educational Testing Service.

Carnevale, A. P., & Rose, S. J. (2004). Socioeconomic status, race/ethnicity, and selective college admissions. In R. D. Kahlenberg (Ed.), *America's untapped resource: Low-income students in higher education* (pp. 101-156). New York, NY: The Century Foundation Press.

Center for Working-Class Studies at Youngstown University. (n.d.). *Teaching.* Retrieved from http://cwcs.ysu.edu/teaching

Chambers, T., & Deller, F. (2011). Chances and choices of low-income students in Canada and England: A post-structuralist discussion of early intervention. In A. Kezar (Ed.), *Recognizing and serving low-income students in higher education: An examination of institutional policies, practices and culture* (pp. 49-71). New York, NY: Routledge Taylor & Francis Group.

Chapman, C., Laird, J., Ifill, N., & Kewal Ramani, A. (2011). *Trends in high school dropout and completion rates in the United States: 1972–2009* (NCES 2012-006). Washington, DC: U.S. Department of Education, National Center for Education Statistics.

Chapman, S. (2004). *Revise A2: Sociology.* London, England: Letts Educational.

Charlesworth, S. J. (2000). *A phenomenology of working class experience.* Cambridge, England: Cambridge University Press.

Chau, J. (2012, February 26). To guide first-generation students, U. of Nebraska reaches into high schools. *Chronicle of Higher Education.* Retrieved from http://chronicle.com/article/To-Guide-First-Generation/130935/

Chetty, R., Hendren, N., Kline, P., Saez, E., & Turner, N. (2014). Is the United States still a land of opportunity? *Recent trends in intergenerational mobility.* (Working Paper 19844). Cambridge, MA: National Bureau of Economic Research.

Child, R. L. (1998). Upward bound students compared to other college-bound students: Profiles of nonacademic characteristics and academic achievement. *Journal of Negro Education, 67*(4), 346-363.

Choy, S. P. (2001). *Students whose parents did not go to college: Postsecondary access, persistence, and attainment* (NCES 2001-126). Washington, DC: U.S. Department of Education, National Center for Education Statistics.

Choy, S. P. (2002). *Access and persistence: Findings from 10 years of longitudinal research on students.* Washington, DC: U.S. Department of Education.

Choy, S. P., & Carroll, C. D. (2003). *How families of low- and middle-income undergraduates pay for college: Full-time dependent students in 1999–2000*. Washington, DC: U.S. Department of Education, National Center for Education Statistics.

Christopher, R. (1993). Teaching working-class literature to mixed audiences. In S. L. Linkon (Ed.), *Teaching working class* (pp. 203-222), Amherst, MA: University of Massachusetts.

Christopher, R. (2002). Rags to riches to suicide: Unhappy narratives of upward mobility. *College Literature, 29*(4), 79-108.

Christopher, R. (2003). Damned if you do, damned if you don't. *Academe, 89*(4), 37-40.

Class Action. (2014). *Telling first gen stories as transformation*. Retrieved from http://www.classism. org/programs/higher-education/digital-storytelling-project

Coffman, C., O'Neil, T., & Starr, B. (2010). An empirical analysis of the impact of legacy preferences on alumni giving at top universities. In R. D. Kahlenberg (Ed.), *Affirmative action for the rich: Legacy preferences in college admissions* (pp. 101-122). New York, NY: The Century Foundation Press.

Cole, E. R., & Omari, S. R. (2003). Race, class, and the dilemmas of upward mobility for African Americans. *Journal of Social Issues, 59*(4), 785-802.

Coleman, J. S. (1988). Social capital in the creation of human capital. *American Journal of Sociology, 94* (Supplement), S95-S120.

College Possible. (2013). *Annual impact report, 2012-2013*. St. Paul, MN: Author.

Collier, P. J., & Morgan, D. L. (2008). "Is that paper really due today?": Differences in first-generation and traditional college students' understandings of faculty expectations. *Higher Education, 55*, 425-446.

Cooke, R., Barkham, M., Audin, K., Bradley, M., & Davy, J. (2004). How social class differences affect students' experience of the university. *Journal of Further and Higher Education, 28*(4), 407-421.

Covarrubias, R., Romero, A., & Trivelli, M. (2014). Family achievement guilt and mental well-being of college students. *Journal of Child and Family Studies*. Advanced online publication. doi: 10.1007/s10826-014-0003-8

Crisp, R. J., & Turner, R. N. (2011). Cognitive adaptation to the experience of social and cultural diversity. *Psychological Bulletin, 137*, 242-266.

Crossley, N. (2008). Social class. In M. Grenfell (Ed.), *Pierre Bourdieu: Key concepts* (pp. 87-99). Stocksfield, UK: Acumen Publishing Limited.

Culver, S. J. (2012, November 11). Let's help students speak up across the cultural divide. *The Chronicle of Higher Education*. Retrieved from www.chronicle.com

Daniels, J. (1998). Class and classroom: Going to work. In A. Shepard, J. McMillan, & G. Tate (Eds.), *Coming to class: Pedagogy and the social class of teachers* (pp. 1-12). Portsmouth, NH: Boynton/ Cook Publishers.

Dartmouth College. (2013). *Past special HOP project: Class divide*. Hopkins Center for the Arts, Dartmouth College. Retrieved from https://hop.dartmouth.edu/Online/class_divide

Delpit, L. (1995). *Other people's children: Cultural conflict in the classroom*. New York, NY: The New Press.

Dennis, J. M., Phinney, J. S., & Chuateco, L. I. (2005). The role of motivation, parental support, and peer support in the academic success of ethnic minority first-generation college students. *Journal of College Student Development, 46*(3), 223-236.

DeSalvo, L. (1998). Digging deep. In A. Shepard, J. McMillan, & G. Tate (Eds.), *Coming to class: Pedagogy and the social class of teachers* (pp. 13-22). Portsmouth, NH: Boynton/Cook Publishers.

Dickbert-Conlin, S., & Rubenstein, R. (2007). Introduction. In S. Dickbert-Conlin & R. Rubenstein (Eds.), *Economic inequality and higher education: Access, persistence, and success* (pp. 1-13). New York, NY: Russell Sage Foundation.

Dougherty, K. J., & Kienzl, G. (2006). It's not enough to get through the open door: Inequalities by social background in transfer from community colleges to four-year colleges. *Sociology of Education, 60,* 86-103.

Dynarski, S. M. (2004). The new merit aid. In C. Hoxby (Ed.), *College choices: The economics of where to go, when to go, and how to pay for it* (pp. 63-100). Chicago, IL: University of Chicago Press.

Ehrenreich, B. (2001). *Nickel and dimed: On (not) getting by in America.* New York, NY: Metropolitan Books.

Elwell, C. K. (2014, March 10). *The distribution of household income and the middle class.* Washington, DC: Federation of American Scientists, Congressional Research Service.

Engle, J. (2007). Postsecondary access and success for first generation college students. *American Academic, 3*(1), 25-48.

Engle, J., & Lynch, M. G. (2011). Demography is not destiny: What colleges and universities can do to improve persistence among low-income students. In A. Kezar (Ed.), *Recognizing and serving low-income students in higher education: An examination of institutional policies, practices, and culture* (pp. 161-175). New York, NY: Routledge.

Engle, J., & O'Brien, C. (2007). *Demography is not destiny: Increasing the graduation rates of low-income college students at large public universities.* Washington, DC: The Pell Institute for the Study of Opportunity in Higher Education.

Engle, J., & Tinto, V. (2008). *Moving beyond access: College for low-income, first-generation students.* Washington, DC: The Pell Institute for the study of Opportunity in Higher Education.

Espinoza, R. (2011). *Pivotal moments: How educators can put all students on the path to college.* Cambridge, MA: Harvard University Press.

Evans, S. (2009). In a different place: Working-class girls and higher education. *Sociology, 43*(2), 340-355.

Finley, A., & McNair, T. (2013). *Assessing underserved students' engagement in high-impact practices.* Washington, DC: Association of American Colleges and Universities.

Fiske, S. T., & Markus, H. R. (2012). *Facing social class: How societal rank influences interaction.* New York, NY: Russell Sage Foundation.

Fullinwider, R. K., & Lichtenberg, J. (2004). *Leveling the playing field: Justice, politics, and college admissions.* Lanham, MD: Rowman & Littlefield.

Galligani Casey, J. (2005). Diversity, discourse, and the working-class student. *Academe, 91*(4), 33-36.

Gilbert, D. (2008). *The American class structure in an age of growing inequality.* Thousand Oaks, CA: Pine Forge Press.

Gittens, C. G. (2014). The McNair program as socializing influence on doctoral degree attainment. *Peabody Journal of Education, 89*(3), 368-379.

Godinez Ballón, E., Chávez, C., Gómez, S. T., & Mizumoto Posey, S. (2006) Are you oppressed if you don't think you are? Defining and defending prosperity among working-class students in a public university. *Women's Studies, 35,* 595-604.

Golden, D. (2006). *The price of admission: How America's ruling class buys its way into elite colleges—and who gets left outside the gates.* New York, NY: Crown Publishers.

Golden, D. (2010). An analytical survey of legacy preference. In R. D. Kahlenberg (Ed.), *Affirmative action for the rich: Legacy preferences in college admissions* (pp. 71-100). New York, NY: The Century Foundation Press.

Goldhaber, D., & Peri, G. K. (2007). Community colleges. In S. Dickert-Conlin & R. Rubenstein (Eds.), *Economic inequality and higher education: Access, persistence, and success* (pp. 101-127). New York, NY: Russell Sage Foundation.

Goldrick-Rab, S. (2006). Following their every move: An investigation of social-class differences in college pathways. *Sociology of Education, 79*(1), 61-79.

Goldthorpe, J. (2007). *On sociology* (2nd ed.). Stanford, CA: Stanford University Press.

Goldthorpe, J., & Jackson, M. (2008). Education-based meritocracy: The barriers to its realization. In A. Lareau & D. Conley (Eds.), *Social class: How does it work?* (pp. 93-117). New York, NY: Russell Sage Foundation.

Gorman, T. J. (2000). Cross-class perceptions of social class. *Sociological Spectrum, 20*(1), 93-120.

Goyette, K. A., & Mullen, A. L. (2006). Who studies the arts and sciences? Social background and the choice and consequences of undergraduate field of study. *Journal of Higher Education, 77*(3), 497-538.

Graham, L. (2011). Learning in a new world: Reflections on being a first-generation college student and the influence of TRIO programs. In V. L. Harvey & T. H. Housel (Eds.), *Faculty and first-generation college students: Bridging the classroom gap together* (New Directions for Teaching and Learning, 127, pp. 33-38). San Francisco, CA: Jossey-Bass.

Graham, L. O. (1999). *Our kind of people: Inside America's Black upper class.* New York, NY: HarperCollins.

Granfield, R. (1991). Making it by faking it: Working-class students in an elite academic environment. *Journal of Contemporary Ethnography, 20*(3), 659-676.

Grassi, E., Armon, J., & Bulmahn Barker, H. (2008). Don't lose your working-class students. *Diversity and Democracy, 11*(3), 4-6.

Green, A. (2003). Learning to tell stories: Social class, narratives, and pedagogy. *Modern Language Studies, 33*(1/2), 80-89.

Greenfield, G. A., Keup, J. R., & Gardner, J. N. (2013). *Developing and sustaining successful first-year programs: A guide for practitioners.* San Francisco, CA: Jossey-Bass.

Grenfell, M. (2004). *Pierre Bourdieu: Agent provocateur.* London, England: Continuum.

Guinier, L., & Sturm, S. (2001). Who's qualified? *A new democracy forum on creating equal opportunity in school and jobs.* Boston, MA: Beacon Press.

Gupton, J. T., Castelo-Rodriguez, C., Martinez, D. A., & Quintanar, I. (2009). Creating a pipeline to engage low-income, first-generation college students. In S. R. Harper & S. J. Quaye (Eds.),

Student engagement in higher education: *Theoretical perspectives and practical approaches to diverse populations* (pp. 243-260). New York, NY: Routledge.

Hale, Jr., F. W. (2004). *What makes racial diversity work in higher education: Academic leaders present successful policies and strategies.* Sterling, VA: Stylus.

Haring-Smith, T. (2012). Broadening our definition of diversity. *Liberal Education, 98*(2), 6-13.

Hart, J., & Hubbard, J. (2010). Consuming higher education: Who is paying the price? In E. J. Allan, S. V. D. Iverson, & R. Ropers-Huilman (Eds.), *Reconstructing policy in higher education: Feminist poststructural perspectives* (pp. 147-165). New York, NY: Routledge.

Haveman, R., & Smeeding, T. (2006). The role of higher education in social mobility. *The Future of Children, 16*(2), 125-150.

Haveman, R., & Wilson, K. (2007). Access, matriculation, and graduation. In S. Dickbert-Conlin & R. Rubenstein (Eds.), *Economic inequality and higher education: Access, persistence, and success* (pp. 17-43). New York, NY: Russell Sage Foundation.

Heller, J. L. (2011). The enduring problem of social class stigma experienced by upwardly mobile White academics. *McGill Sociological Review, 2,* 19-38.

Hess, S. M. (2007). Navigating class on campus: *The peer culture of working-class undergraduates.* (Doctoral dissertation). Retrieved from ProQuest Dissertations and Theses database. (AAT 3268505)

Higbee, J. L., & Goff, E. (2008). *Pedagogy and student services for institutional transformation: Implementing universal design in higher education.* Minneapolis, MN: Center for Research on Developmental Education and Urban Literacy, University of Minnesota.

Hodges, T. D., & Clifton, D. O. (2004). Strengths-based development in practice. In P. A. Linley & S. Joseph (Eds.), *Positive psychology in practice: From research to application* (pp. 256-268). New York, NY: John Wiley and Sons.

hooks, b. (2000). *Where we stand: Class matters.* New York, NY: Routledge.

Horn, L. J., Chen, X., & Chapman, C. (2003). *Getting ready to pay for college: What students and their parents know about the cost of college tuition and what they are doing to find out.* Washington, DC: U. S. Department of Education.

Horn, L., & Nunez, A. (2000). *Mapping the road to college: First-generation students' math track, planning strategies, and context of support.* Washington, DC: U.S. Department of Education, National Center for Education Statistics.

Horvat, E. M. (2001). Understanding equity and access in higher education: The potential contribution of Pierre Bourdieu. In J. C. Smart (Ed.), *Higher education: Handbook of theory and practice* (pp. 195-238). New York, NY: Agathon.

Hurst, A. L. (2010). *The burden of academic success: Managing working-class identities while in college.* New York, NY: Rowman & Littlefield.

Hurst, A. L. (2012). *College and the working class: What it takes to make it.* Rotterdam, The Netherlands: Sense Publishers.

Immerwahr, J., Johnson, J., Ott, A. B., & Rochkind, J. (2010). *Squeeze play 2010: Continued public anxiety on cost, harsher judgments on how colleges are run.* San Jose, CA: National Center for Public Policy and Higher Education.

Inkelas, K. K., Daver, Z. E., Vogt, K. E., & Leonard, J. B. (2007). Living-learning programs and first-generation college students' academic and social transition to college. *Research in Higher Education, 48*(4), 403-434.

Ishitani, T. T. (2006). Studying attrition and degree completion behavior among first-generation college students in the United States. *Journal of Higher Education, 77,* 861-885.

Jehangir, R. R. (2010). *Higher education and first-generation students: Cultivating community, voice, and place for the new majority.* New York, NY: Palgrave McMillan.

Jenkins, A. L., Miyazaki, Y., & Janosik, S. M. (2009). Predictors that distinguish first-generation college students from non-first-generation college students. *Journal of Multicultural, Gender, and Minority Studies, 3*(1), 1-9.

Jensen, B. (2004). Across the great divide: Crossing classes and clashing cultures. In M. Zweig (Ed.), *What's class got to do with it?* (pp. 168-184). Ithaca, NY: Cornell University Press.

Jensen, B. (2012). *Reading classes: On culture and classism in America.* Ithaca, NY: Cornell University Press.

Johnson, D. W., Johnson, R. T., & Smith, K. A. (1998). Cooperative learning returns to college: What evidence is there that it works? *Change, 30*(4), 26-35.

Johnson, J., Rochkind, J., Ott, A. N., & DuPont, S. (2010). *Can I get a little advice here? How an over-stretched high school guidance system is undermining students' college aspirations.* New York, NY: Public Agenda.

Jonas, S. (1999). Population data for health and health care. In A. R. Kovner, & S. Jonas (Eds.), *Health care delivery in the United States* (6th ed., pp. 7-13). New York, NY: Springer.

Jones, S., & Vagle, M. D. (2013). Living contradictions and working for change: Toward a theory of social class-sensitive pedagogy. *Educational Researcher, 42*(3), 129-141.

Kahlenberg, R. D. (2010). Introduction. In R. D. Kahlenberg (Ed.), *Affirmative action for the rich: Legacy preferences in college admissions* (pp. 1-18). New York, NY: The Century Foundation Press.

Kahlenberg, R. D. (2013, February 11). How much do you pay for college? *The Chronicle of Higher Education.* Retrieved from www.chronicle.com.

Kane, T. J. (2004). College going inequality. In K. Neckerman (Ed.), *Social inequality* (pp. 319-354). New York, NY: Russell Sage Foundation.

Kantrowitz, M. (2009). *Analysis of why some students do not apply for financial aid.* Retrieved from http://www.finaid.org/educators/20090427CharacteristicsOfNonApplicants.pdf.

Karabel, J. (2005). *The chosen: The hidden history of admission and exclusion at Harvard, Yale, and Princeton.* Boston, MA: Houghton Mifflin.

Keaton, P. (2012). *Public elementary and secondary school student enrollment and staff counts from the common core of data: School year 2010-2011* (NCES 2012-327). U.S. Department of Education, National Center for Education Statistics.

Kezar, A. (2000). *Summer bridge programs: Supporting all students.* Washington, DC: ERIC Clearinghouse on Higher Education, George Washington University. (ERIC Digest No. ED 442 421)

Kezar, A. (Ed.). (2011). *Recognizing and serving low-income students in higher education: An examination of institutional policies, practices, and culture.* New York, NY: Routledge.

King, C. S. (2012). What's a nice girl like you doing in a place this like? *Journal of Public Affairs Education, 18*(1), 51-66.

King, J. E. (2005). Academic success and financial decisions: Helping students make crucial choices. In R. S. Feldman (Ed.), *Improving the first year of college: Research and practice* (pp. 3-25). Mahwah, NJ: Lawrence Erlbaum.

King, J. E. (2006). *Missed opportunities revisited: New information on students who do not apply for financial aid.* Washington, DC: American Council on Education.

Kuh, G. D. (2008). *High-impact educational practices: What they are, who has access to them, and why they matter.* Washington, DC: Association of American Colleges and Universities.

Kulm, T. L., & Cramer, S. (2006). The relationship of student employment to student role, family relationships, social interactions, and persistence. *College Student Journal, 40*(4), 927-939.

Kuriloff, P., & Reichert, M. C. (2003). Boys of class, boys of color: Negotiating the academic and social geography of an elite independent school. *Journal of Social Issues, 59*(4), 751-769.

Langhout, R. D., Rosselli, F., & Feinstein, J. (2007). Assessing classism in academic settings. *The Review of Higher Education, 30,* 145-184.

Lareau, A. (2003). *Unequal childhoods: Class, race, and family life.* Berkeley, CA: University of California Press.

Lehman, J. S. (2004). The evolving language of diversity and integration in discussions of affirmative action from *Bakke* to *Grutter.* In P. Gurin, J. S. Lehman, & E. Lewis (Eds.), *Defending diversity: Affirmative action at the University of Michigan* (pp. 61-96). Ann Arbor, MI: University of Michigan Press.

Lehmann, W. (2004). "For some reason I get a little scared": Structure, agency, and risk in school-work transitions. *Journal of Youth Studies, 7*(4), 379-396.

Lehmann, W. (2007). "I just didn't feel like I fit in": The role of habitus in university drop-out decisions. *Canadian Journal of Higher Education, 37*(2), 89-110.

Lehmann, W. (2009). Becoming middle class: How working-class university students draw and transgress moral class boundaries. *Sociology, 43*(4), 631-647.

Lehmann, W. (2013). Habitus transformation and hidden injuries: Successful working-class university students. *Sociology of Education.* Advanced online publication. doi: 10.1177/0038040713498777

Leigh, D. E., & Gill, A. M. (2003). Do community colleges really divert students from earning bachelor's degrees? *Economics of Education Review, 22*(1), 23-30.

Leonhardt, D. (2004, April 22). As wealthy fill top colleges, concerns grow over fairness. *New York Times,* p. A1.

Levine, A., & Dean, D. R. (2012). *Generation on a tightrope: A portrait of today's college student.* San Francisco, CA: Jossey-Bass.

Lind, M. (2010). Legacy preferences in a democratic republic. In R. D. Kahlenberg (Ed.), *Affirmative action for the rich: Legacy preferences in college admissions* (pp. 21-31). New York, NY: The Century Foundation Press.

Lindquist, J. (2002). *A place to stand: Politics and persuasion in a working-class bar.* Oxford, UK: Oxford University Press.

Linkon, S. L. (2008). Stratified learning: Responding to the class system of higher education. *Diversity & Democracy, 11,* 10-11.

Lippincott, J. A., & German, N. (2007). From blue collar to ivory tower: Counseling first-generation, working-class students. In J. A. Lippincott & R. B. Lippincott (Eds.), *Special populations in college counseling: A handbook for mental health professionals* (pp. 89-98). Alexandria, VA: American Counseling Association.

Long, B. T. (2008). *What is known about the impact of financial aid?: Implications for policy.* (A NCRP Working Paper). New York, NY: National Center for Postsecondary Research. Retrieved from http://www.postsecondaryresearch.org/i/a/document/6963_LongFinAid.pdf

Longwell-Grice, R. (2003). Get a job: Working class students discuss the purpose of college. *College Student Affairs Journal, 23*(1), 40-53.

Longwell-Grice, R., & Longwell-Grice, H. (2007-2008). Testing Tinto: How do retention theories work for first-generation, working-class students? *Journal of College Student Retention: Research, Theory and Practice, 9,* 407-420.

Lott, B. (2002). Cognitive and behavioral distancing from the poor. *American Psychologist, 57*(2), 100-110.

Lott, B., & Bullock, H. E. (2007). *Psychology and economic injustice: Personal, professional, and political intersections.* Washington, DC: American Psychological Association.

Lubrano, A. (2004). *Limbo: Blue-collar roots, white-collar dreams.* Hoboken, NJ: John Wiley & Sons.

Lucey, H., Melody, J., & Walkerdine, V. (2003). Uneasy hybrids: Psychosocial aspects of becoming educationally successful for working-class young women. *Gender and Education, 15*(3), 285-299.

MacKenzie, L. (1998). A pedagogy of respect: Teaching as an ally of working-class college students. In A. Shepard, J. McMillan, & G. Tate (Eds.), *Coming to class: Pedagogy and the social class of teachers* (pp. 94-116). Portsmouth, NH: Boynton/Cook Publishers.

Martin, G. L. (2012). *Getting out, missing out, and surviving: The social class experiences of White, low-income, first-generation college students* (Doctoral dissertation). University of Iowa. Retrieved from http://ir.uiowa.edu/etd/2937/

Martin, J. (2008). Pedagogy of the alienated: Can Freirian teaching reach working-class students? *Equity & Excellence in Education, 41*(1), 31-44.

Martinez, J. A., Sher, K. J., Krull, J. L., & Wood, P. K. (2009). Blue-collar scholars? Mediators and moderators of university attrition in first-generation college students. *Journal of College Student Development, 50*(1), 87-103.

Maton, K. (2008). Habitus. In M. Grenfell (Ed.), *Pierre Bourdieu: Key concepts* (pp. 49-66). Stocksfield, UK: Acumen Publishing Limited.

Matthys, M. (2013). *Cultural capital, identity, and social mobility: The life course of working-class university graduates.* (N. Perlzweig, Trans.). New York, NY: Routledge.

Mayhew, M. J., & Fernandez, S. D. (2007). Pedagogical practices that contribute to social justice outcomes. *The Review of Higher Education, 31*(1), 55-80.

McDaniels, A., Hyatt, A., Androphy, D., Cummings, D., Cabrera, D., & Mateo, K. (2014, February 17). More than a theme, not just a costume [Guest column]. *The Daily Pennsylvanian.* Retrieved from http://www.thedp.com/article/2014/02/more-than-theme

McDonough, P. M. (1997). *Choosing colleges: How social class and schools structure opportunity.* Albany, NY: State University of New York Press.

McDonough, P. M. (2005). Counseling and college counseling in America's high schools. In D. A. Hawkins & J. Lautz (Eds.), *State of college admission* (pp. 107–121). Washington, DC: National Association for College Admission Counseling.

McDonough, P. M., Ventresca, M., & Outcault, C. (2000). Field of dreams: Organizational field approaches to understanding the transformation of college access, 1965-1995. In J. Smart (Ed.), *Higher education: Handbook of theory and research* (Vol. 15, pp. 371-405). Edison, NJ: Agathon Press.

McLoughlin, P. J. (2012). The transition experiences of high-achieving, low-income undergraduates in an elite college environment. *Journal of The First-Year Experience & Students in Transition, 24*(2), 9-32.

McNamee, S. J., & Miller, Jr., R. K. (2014). *The meritocracy myth* (3rd ed.). Lanham, MD: Rowman & Littlefield.

Miller, S. (2013, May 17). New RSO lays out class divide. *The Chicago Maroon.* Retrieved from http://chicagomaroon.com/2013/05/17/new-rso-lays-out-class-divide/

Mohr, J., & DiMaggio, P. (1995). The intergenerational transmission of cultural capital. *Research in Social Stratification and Mobility, 14,* 167-199.

Morales, E. E. (2014). Learning from success: How original research on academic resilience informs what college faculty can do to increase the retention of low socioeconomic status students. *International Journal of Higher Education, 3*(3), 92-102.

Morris, E. W. (2005). From "middle class" to "trailer trash:" Teachers' perceptions of White students in a predominately minority school. *Sociology of Education, 78,* 99-121.

Mortenson, T. G. (2010). Family income and educational attainment 1970 to 2009. *Postsecondary Education Opportunity, 221,* 1-16.

Museus, S. D., & Griffin, K. A. (2011). Mapping the margins in higher education: On the promise of intersectionality frameworks in research and discourse. In K. A. Griffin & S. D. Museus (Eds.), *Using mixed-methods approaches to study intersectionality in higher education* (New Directions for Institutional Research, No. 151, pp. 5-14). San Francisco, CA: Jossey-Bass.

Muzzatti, S. L., & Samarco, C. V. (Eds.). (2006). *Reflections from the wrong side of the tracks.* New York, NY: Rowan & Littlefield.

Myers, D. E., & Schirm, A. L. (1999). *The impacts of Upward Bound: Final report for phase I of the national evaluation. Executive Summary.* (Contract No. LC-92001001; MPR Reference No. 8046-515). Washington, DC: U.S. Department of Education, Planning and Evaluation Services.

National Center for Education Statistics. (2008). *National Postsecondary Student Aid Study (NPSAS).* Washington, DC: U.S. Department of Education.

National Opinion Research Center (NORC). (2007). *Survey of Earned Doctorates.* Chicago, IL: University of Chicago. Retrieved from http://www.norc.org/Research/Projects/Pages/survey-of-earned-doctorates-%28sed%29.aspx

The New York Times. (2005). *Class matters.* New York, NY: Times Books.

Norton, M. I., & Ariely, D. (2001). Building a better America one wealth quantile at a time. *Perspectives on Psychological Science, 6,* 9-12.

Oakes, J. (2008). Keeping track: Structuring equality and inequality in an era of accountability. *Teachers College Record, 110*(3), 700-712.

Oakes, J., & Saunders, M. (Eds.). (2008). *Beyond tracking: Multiple pathways to college, career, and civic participation.* Cambridge, MA: Harvard Education Press.

Office for National Statistics. (2010). *SOC2010 Volume 3: The National Statistics socio-economic classification* (NS-SEC rebased on the SOC2010). South Wales, UK: Author.

Oldfield, K. (2012). Still humble and hopeful: Two more recommendations on welcoming first-generation poor and working-class students to college. *About Campus, 17*(5), 2-13.

Oldfield, K., & Conant, R. F. (2001). Professors, social class, and affirmative action. *Journal of Public Affairs Education, 7*(2), 171-185.

Ornstein, A. (2007). *Class counts: Education, inequality, and the shrinking middle class.* New York, NY: Rowman & Littlefield Publishers.

Ortiz, A. (2004). Promoting the success of Latino students: A call to action. In A. Ortiz (Ed.), *Addressing the unique needs of Latino American student* (New Directions for Student Services, No. 105, pp. 89-970). San Francisco, CA: Jossey-Bass.

Ostrove, J. M. (2003). Belonging and wanting: Meanings of social class background for women's constructions of their college experiences. *Journal of Social Issues, 59*(4), 771-784.

Ostrove, J. M. (2007). Social class and belonging: Implications for college adjustment. *The Review of Higher Education, 30*(4), 363-389.

Ostrove, J. M., & Cole, E. R. (2003). Privileging class: Toward a critical pedagogy of social class in the context of education. *Journal of Social Issues, 59,* 677-692.

Pallais, A., & Turner, S. E. (2007). Access to elites. In S. Dickbert-Conlin & R. Rubenstein (Eds.), *Economic inequality and higher education: Access, persistence, and success* (pp. 128-156). New York, NY: Russell Sage Foundation.

Pascarella, E. T., & Terenzini, P. T. (2005). *How college affects students: Vol. 2. A third decade of research.* San Francisco, CA: Jossey-Bass.

Patton, L. D. (2006). The voice of reason: A qualitative examination of Black student perceptions of Black culture centers. *Journal of College Student Development, 47,* 628-646.

Paulsen, M. B., & St. John, E. P. (2002). Social class and college costs: Examining the nexus between college choice and persistence. *The Journal of Higher Education, 73*(2), 189-236.

Payne, R. K. (2005). *A framework for understanding poverty* (4th ed.). Highlands, TX: aha! process.

Pearce, J., Down, B., & Moore, E. (2008). Social class, identity and the "good" student: Negotiating university culture. *Australian Journal of Education, 52*(3), 257-271.

Perna, L. W., & Hadinger, M. A. (2012). Promoting academic capital formation among urban youth: Citywide approaches. In R. Winkle-Wagner, P. J. Bowman, & E. P. St. John (Eds.), *Expanding postsecondary opportunity for underrepresented students: Theory and practice of academic capital formation. Readings on equal education* (Vol. 26, pp. 29-64). New York, NY: AMS Press.

Perna, L. W., Lundy-Wagner, V., Yee, A., Brill, L., & Tadal, T. (2011). Showing them the money: The role of institutional financial aid policies and communication strategies in attracting low-income students. In A. Kezar (Ed.), *Recognizing and serving low-income students in higher education: An examination of institutional policies, practices and culture* (pp. 72-96). New York, NY: Routledge Taylor & Francis Group.

Plummer, G. (2000). *Failing working-class girls*. Stoke-on-Trent, UK: Trentham.

Potter, H. (2014). Transitioning to race-neutral admissions: An overview of experiences in states where affirmative action has been banned. In R. D. Kahlenberg (Ed.), *The future of affirmative action: New paths to higher education diversity after Fisher v. University of Texas* (pp. 75-90). New York, NY: The Century Foundation Press.

Public Broadcasting Service. (2001). *People like us: Social class in America* (companion website). Retrieved from http://www.pbs.org/peoplelikeus/

Putnam, R. D. (2001). *Bowling alone: The collapse and revival of American community*. New York, NY: Simon & Schuster.

Quinn, J. (2004). Understanding working-class "drop-out" from higher education through a sociocultural lens: Cultural narratives and local contexts. *International Studies in Sociology of Education, 14*(1), 57-73.

Reay, D. (1997). The double bind of the working class feminist academic: The success of failure or the failure of success? In P. Mahony & C. Zmroczek (Eds.), *Class matters: Working class women's perspectives on social class* (pp. 19-30). London, England: Taylor & Francis.

Reay, D., Crozier, G., & Clayton, J. (2009). Strangers in paradise? Working-class students in elite universities. *Sociology, 43*(6), 1103-1121.

Reay, D., David, M., & Ball, S. (2001). Making a difference? Institutional habituses and higher education choice. *Sociological Research Online, 5*(4). Retrieved from http://www.socresonline.org.uk/5/4/reay.html

Reay, D., David, M., & Ball, S. (2005). *Degrees of choice: Class, race, gender, and higher education*. Stoke-on-Trent, England: Trentham Books.

Reay, D., Davies, J., David, M., & Ball, S. J. (2001). Choices of degree or degrees of choice? Class, "race" and the higher education choice process. *Sociology, 35*(4), 855-874.

Robbins, S. B., Le, H., Davis, D., Lauver, K., Langley, R., & Calstrom, A. (2004). Do psychosocial and study skill factors predict college outcomes? A meta-analysis. *Psychological Bulletin, 130,* 261-288.

Rollock, N., Vincent, C., Gillborn, D., & Ball, S. (2012). "Middle class by profession": Class status and identification amongst the Black middle classes. *Ethnicities, 13*(3), 253-275.

Rose, M. (2004). *The mind at work: Valuing the intelligence of the American worker*. New York, NY: Viking Press.

Rubenstein, R., & Scafidi, B. (2002). Who pays and who benefits? Examining the distributional consequences on the Georgia Lottery for education. *National Tax Journal, 55*(2), 223-238.

Rubin, M. (2012a). Social class differences in social integration among students in higher education: A meta-analysis and recommendations for future research. *Journal of Diversity in Higher Education, 5*(1), 22-38.

Rubin, M. (2012b). Working-class students need more friends at university: A cautionary note for Australia's higher education equity initiative. *Higher Education Research & Development, 31*(3), 431-433.

Rubin, M., Denson, N., Kilpatrick, S., Matthews, K. E., Stehlik, T., & Zyngier, D. (2014). "I am working-class": Subjective self-definition as a missing measure of social class and socioeconomic status in higher education research. *Educational Researcher, 43*(4), 196-200.

Ryan, J., & Sackrey, C. (1984). *Strangers in paradise: Academics from the working class.* Boston, MA: South End Press.

Sacks, P. (1999). *Standardized minds: The high price of America's testing culture and what we can do to change it.* Cambridge, MA: Perseus Press.

Sacks, P. (2001, April 2). SAT—A failing test. *The Nation, 272*(13), 7.

Sacks, P. (2007). *Tearing down the gates: Confronting the class divide in American education.* Berkeley, CA: University of California Press.

Schmidt, P. (2010, September 19). *Working-class students band together at the U. of Wisconsin. Chronicle of Higher Education.* Retrieved from http://chronicle.com/article/Working-Class-Students-Band/124448/

Schreiner, L. A. (2013). Strengths-based advising. In J. K. Drake, P. Jordan, & M. A. Miller (Eds.), *Academic advising approaches: Strategies that teach students to make the most of college* (pp. 105-120). San Francisco, CA: Jossey-Bass.

Schwartz, J. L., Donovan, J., & Guido-DiBrito, F. (2009). Stories of social class: Self-identified Mexican male college students crack the silence. *Journal of College Student Development, 50*(1), 50-66.

Seider, M. (2008). The dynamics of social reproduction: How class works at a state college and private elite college. *Equity and Excellence in Education, 41*(1), 45-61.

Shook, J. L., & Keup, J. R. (2012). The benefits of peer leader programs: An overview from the literature. In J. R. Keup (Ed.), *Peer leadership in higher education* (New Directions for Higher Education, 157, pp. 5-16). San Francisco, CA: Jossey-Bass.

Shor, I. (2005). Why teach about social class? *Teaching English in the Two-Year College, 33,* 161-170.

Shott, M. J. (2006). How liberal arts colleges perpetuate class bias. *Academe, 92*(5), 22-25.

Silva, J. M. (2012). Constructing adulthood in an age of uncertainty. *American Sociological Review, 77*(4), 505-522.

Smith, B. (2007). Accessing social capital through the academic mentoring process. *Equity and Excellence in Education, 40*(1), 36-46.

Smith, B. (2013). *Mentoring at-risk students through the hidden curriculum of higher education.* Lanham, MD: Lexington Books.

Soria, K. M. (2012). Creating a successful transition for working-class first-year students. *The Journal of College Orientation and Transition, 20*(1), 44-55.

Soria, K. M. (2013a, February). *High-impact practices: Implications for transfer students' intellectual and interpersonal development.* Paper presented at the National Institute for the Study of Transfer Students, Dallas, TX.

Soria, K. M. (2013b). Social class reconsidered: Examining the role of class and privilege in fraternities and sororities. *Association of Fraternity and Sorority Advisors, AFA Essentials,* 1-4.

Soria, K. M. (2013c). *What happens outside of the college class(ed)room? Examining college students' social class and social integration in higher education.* (Doctoral dissertation). Retrieved from ProQuest. (3567476).

Soria, K. M., & Barratt, W. (2012, June). *Examining class in the classroom: Utilizing social class data in institutional and academic research.* Paper presented at the Association for Institutional Research Forum, New Orleans, LA.

Soria, K. M., & Bultmann, M. (2014). Advising scholars from blue collar backgrounds: Supporting working-class students' success in higher education. *NACADA Journal, 34*(2), 51-62.

Soria, K. M., Hussein, D., & Vue, C. (2014). Leadership for whom? Socioeconomic factors predicting undergraduate students' positional leadership participation. *Journal of Leadership Education, 13*(1), 14-30.

Soria, K. M., Lingren Clark, B., & Coffin Koch, L. (2013). Investigating the academic and social benefits of extended new student orientations for first-year students. *The Journal of College Orientation and Transition, 20*(2), 33-45.

Soria, K. M., & Stebleton, M. J. (2012). First-generations students' academic engagement and retention. *Teaching in Higher Education, 17*(6), 673-685.

Soria, K. M., & Stebleton, M. J. (2013). Social capital, academic engagement, and sense of belonging among working-class college students. *College Student Affairs Journal, 31*(2), 139-153.

Soria, K. M., Stebleton, M. J., & Huesman, R. L. (2013-2014). Class counts: Exploring differences in academic and social integration between working-class and middle/upper-class students at large, public research universities. *Journal of College Student Retention: Research, Theory, and Practice, 15*(2), 215-242.

Soria, K. M., & Stubblefield, R. (2014). First-year college students' strengths awareness: Building a foundation for student engagement and academic excellence. *Journal of The First-Year Experience & Students in Transition, 26*(2), 69-88.

Soria, K. M., & Stubblefield, R. (in press). Knowing me, knowing you: Building strengths awareness and belonging in higher education. *Journal of College Student Retention: Research, Theory, and Practice.*

Soria, K. M., Weiner, B., & Lu, E. C. (2014). Examining financial decisions among undergraduate students from different social class backgrounds. *Journal of Student Financial Aid, 44*(1), 2-23.

Soto, R. (2008). Race and class: Taking action at the intersections. *Diversity & Democracy, 11,* 12-13.

St. John, E. P., & Chung, A. S. (2007). Access to advanced math. In E. P. St. John (Ed.), *Education and the special interest: School reform, public finance, and access to higher education* (pp. 135-162). New York, NY: Springer.

St. John, E. P., Hu, S., & Fisher, A. S. (2011). *Breaking through the access barrier: How academic capital formation can improve policy in higher education.* New York, NY: Routledge.

Stampnitzky, L. (2006). How does "culture" become "capital"? Cultural and institutional struggles over character and personality at Harvard. *Sociological Perspective, 49,* 461-481.

Stanton-Salazar, R. D. (1997). A social capital framework for understanding the socialization of racial minority youth. *Harvard Educational Review, 67*(1), 1-40.

Stephens, N. M., Fryberg, S. A., Markus, H. R., Johnson, C., & Covarrubias, R. (2012). Unseen disadvantage: How American universities' focus on independence undermines the academic performance of first-generation college students. *Journal of Personality and Social Psychology, 102,* 1178-1197.

Stephens, N. M., Hamedani, M. G., & Destin, M. (2014). Closing the social-class achievement gap: A difference-education intervention improves first-generation students' academic performance and all students' college transition. *Psychological Science.* Advanced online publication. doi: 10.1177/0956797613518349

Stephens, N. M., Townsend, S. S. M., Markus, H. R., & Phillips, L. T. (2012). A cultural mismatch: Independent cultural norms produce greater increases in cortisol and more negative emotions among first-generation college students. *Journal of Experimental Social Psychology, 48*(6), 1389–1393.

Stevens, M. L. (2007). *Creating a class: College admissions and the education of elites.* Cambridge, MA: Harvard University Press.

Stuber, J. (2006). Talk of class: Discursive repertoires of white working- and upper-middle class college students. *Journal of Contemporary Ethnography, 35*, 285- 318.

Stuber, J. (2011). *Inside the college gates: How class and culture matter in higher education.* Lanham, MD: Rowman and Littlefield.

Sullivan, A. (2001). Cultural capital and educational attainment. *Sociology, 35*(4), 893-912.

Sullivan, N. (2003). Academic constructions of "White trash," or how to insult poor people without really trying. In V. C. Adair & S. L. Dahlberg (Eds.), *Reclaiming class* (pp. 53-66). Philadelphia, PA: Temple University Press.

Teixeria, R., & Abramowitz, A. (2008). *The decline of the White working class and the rise of a mass upper middle class* (Brookings Working Paper). Washington, DC: Brookings Institution.

Terenzini, P. T., Cabrera, A. F., & Bernal, E. M. (2001). *Swimming against the tide: The poor in American higher education.* Princeton, NJ: College Board.

Terenzini, P. T., Rendon, L., Upcraft, M. L., Millar, S., Allison, K., Gregg, P., & Jalomo, R. (1996). The transition to college: Diverse students, diverse stories. In F. Stage, G. Anya, J. Bean, D. Hossler, & G. Kuh (Eds.), *ASHE Reader on college students: The evolving nature of research* (pp. 54-79). Needham Heights, MA: Ginn Press.

Tett, L. (2000). "I'm working class and proud of it"—Gendered experiences of non-traditional participants in higher education. *Gender and Education, 12*(2), 183-194.

Tienda, M. (2013). Diversity ≠ inclusion: Promoting integration in higher education. *Educational Researcher, 42*(9), 467-475.

Tierney, W. G., & Venegas, K. M. (2006). Fictive kin and social capital: The role of peer groups in applying and paying for college. *American Behavioral Scientist, 49*, 1687-1702.

Tinto, V. (1993). *Leaving college: Rethinking the causes and cures of student attrition* (2nd ed.). Chicago, IL: University of Chicago Press.

Tinto, V. (2006). Research and practice of student retention. What's next? *Journal of College Student Retention, 8*(1), 1-19.

Tinto, V. (2012). *Completing college: Rethinking institutional action.* Chicago, IL: University of Chicago Press.

Twenge, J. M., & Campbell, W. K. (2002). Self-esteem & socioeconomic status: A meta-analytic review. *Personality and Social Psychology Review, 6*(1), 59-71.

University of South Carolina. (2015). *SG program collects professional attire for students.* Retrieved from http://www.sc.edu/uofsc/announcements/2015/02_donate_gently_used_professional_attire_rental_program.php#.VQBkd2TF-Nu

University of Wisconsin at River Falls. (2014). *Textbook services.* Retrieved from http://www.uwrf.edu/TextbookServices/FAQ.cfm

Ursinus College. (2014). *Laptop program*. Retrieved from http://ursinus.edu/netcommunity/page. aspx?pid=467

U.S. Census Bureau. (2012). *Annual social and economic supplement to the current population survey*. Washington, DC: Author.

U.S. Department of Labor. (2011). *Women in the labor force: A databook*. Washington, DC: U. S. Government Printing Office.

Vagle, M. D., & Jones, S. (2012). The precarious nature of social class-sensitivity in literacy: A social, autobiographic, and pedagogical project. *Curriculum Inquiry, 42*(3), 318-339.

Vallejo, J. A. (2012). Socially mobile Mexican Americans and the minority culture of mobility. *American Behavioral Scientist, 56*(5), 666-681.

Vander Putten, J. (2001). Bringing social class to the diversity challenge. *About Campus, 6*(5)14-19.

Van Galen, J. A., & Noblit, G. W. (2007). *Late to class: Social class and schooling in the new economy*. Albany, NY: University of New York Press.

Wagoner, T., Schwalbe, A., Hoover, S., & Ernst, D. (2012). *CEHD iPad initiative*. Minneapolis, MN: College of Education and Human Development, University of Minnesota.

Walpole, M. (2003). Socioeconomic status and college: How SES affects college experiences and outcomes. *The Review of Higher Education, 27*, 45-73.

Walpole, M. (2007). *Economically and educationally challenged students in higher education: Access to outcomes* (ASHE Higher Education Report No. 33.3). San Francisco, CA: Jossey-Bass.

Walpole, M. (2011). Academics, campus administration, and social interaction: Examining campus structure using post-structural theory. In A. Kezar (Ed.), *Recognizing and serving low-income students in higher education: An examination of institutional policies, practices, and culture* (pp. 99-120). New York, NY: Routledge Taylor & Francis Group.

Warburton, E. C., Bugarin, R., & Nunez, A. (2001). *Bridging the gap: Academic preparation and post-secondary success of first-generation students*. Washington, DC: U.S. Department of Education, National Center for Education Statistics.

Ward, M. R. M. (2014). "I'm a geek I am": Academic achievement and the performance of a studious working-class masculinity. *Gender and Education, 26*(7), 709-725.

Ward-Roof, J. A. (Ed.). (2010). *Designing successful transitions: A guide for orienting students to college* (Monograph No. 13, 3rd ed.). Columbia, SC: University of South Carolina, National Resource Center for The First-Year Experience and Students in Transition.

Warnock, D. M. (2014). On the other side of what tracks? The missing discussion of social class in the academy. *Rhizomes, 27*. Retrieved from http://rhizomes.net/issue27/warnock.html

Warnock, D. M., & Appel, S. (2012). Learning the unwritten rules: Working class students in graduate school. *Innovative Higher Education, 37*(4), 307-321.

Wilson, J. L. (2002). Blue ring around a white collar: An application of marginality. *ETC: A Review of General Semantics, 59*(1), 25-31.

Winkle-Wagner, R. (2009). *The unchosen me: Race, gender, and identity among Black women in college*. Baltimore, MD: Johns Hopkins University Press.

Winkle-Wagner, R. (2010). *Cultural capital: The promises and pitfalls in educational research.* (ASHE Higher Education Report, 32.1). San Francisco, CA: Jossey-Bass.

Winkle-Wagner, R. (2012). Academic capital formation: Can it help untangle confusion about social stratification in the study of college students? In R. Winkle-Wagner, P. J. Bowman, & E. P. St. John (Eds.), *Expanding postsecondary opportunity for underrepresented students: Theory and practice of academic capital formation. Readings on equal education* (Vol. 26, pp. 293-307). New York, NY: AMS Press.

Winkle-Wagner, R., Bowman, P. J., & St. John, E. P. (Eds.). (2012). *Expanding postsecondary opportunity for underrepresented students: Theory and practice of academic capital formation. Readings on equal education* (Vol. 26). New York, NY: AMS Press.

Witkow, M. R., Gillen-O'Neel, C., & Fuligni, A. J. (2012). College student engagement and school identification: Differences by college type and ethnicity. *Journal of Applied Developmental Psychology, 33*(5), 243-251.

Zandy, J. (1998). The job, the job: The risk of work and the uses of texts. In A. Shepard, J. McMillan, & G. Tate (Eds.), *Coming to class: Pedagogy and the social class of teachers* (pp. 291-308). Portsmouth, NH: Boynton/Cook.

Zimdars, A., Sullivan, A., & Heath, A. (2009). Elite higher education admissions in the arts and sciences: Is cultural capital the key? *Sociology, 43*(4), 648-666.

Zweig, M. (2000). *The working-class majority: America's best kept secret.* Ithaca, NY: Cornell University Press.

Index

A

academic capital and success, 17–18, 34, 53–54
Adelman, Clifford, 20
admissions policies. see college choice and college admission
Aries, Elizabeth, 44, 46, 60, 65
Armstrong, Elizabeth A., 46, 57
attitudes, personal. see habitus

B

Balz, Frank J., 26
Banks, Cerri, 65
Barratt, Will, 17
Baxter, Arthur, 44
Beegle, Donna M., 58, 65
Bourdieu, Pierre, 11–17, 23
Brill, Leykia, 56
Britton, Carolyn, 44
Bryan, Elizabeth, 60

C

Carnevale, Anthony P., 22
Center for Working-Class Studies, 38
Chetty, Raj, 8
classism and racism, 4, 53, 64–65, 67
Coffman, Chad, 24
Coleman, James, 17
college choice and college admission, 21–24. see also finance and financial aid issues
 admissions policies, 24, 54–55
 early decision, 24
 hidden curriculum and, 32–34
 impact of choice, 13–14
college completion
 degree attainment rates, 26–27
 graduation rates, 15
 social integration, importance of, 51
 working-class students and, 1

college experience
 academic support of peers, 47–48, 50
 Class Action and positive self-image, 64
 collaborative and collective pedagogies, 40–41
 faculty relationships, 50
 first-year seminars, 40
 hidden curriculum of, 32–34
 mentors, advice from, 61
 orientation and transition programs, 61
 private college, 44–45
 reframing for success, 38
 strength-based advising, 63
 transfer students, missed opportunities, 36
College Possible, 55
contextual environment. see field
cooperative learning. see college experience
cross-group interaction, 51
cultural capital, 15–17
 benefit of college experience, 46
 comfort level in higher education institutions, 43
 hidden curriculum and, 32–34
 understanding of, 65
Culver, C.J., 39

D

Daniels, Joan E., 44
Dickbert-Conlin, Stacy, 25

E

early admission. see college choice and college admission, admissions policies
Educational Talent Search, 59
Espinoza, Roberta, 53, 58
Esten, Melanie, 26
extracurricular activities and organizations, 47–48

F

faculty
  critical pedagogy, 37
  engagement with working-class
    students, 37
faculty and staff
  diversity awareness, 65
  engagement with working-class students, 39
  family and community, anti-intellectualism
    of, 30–31
field, 12–14
finance and financial aid issues
  college choice and, 25
  cost of higher education, 25
  cultural differences and, 45–46
  easing expenses, 57
  housing and meal plan costs, 57
  informational assistance, 53, 55, 56
  need-based, benefits of, 56–57
  networking and, 48
  study abroad and internships and, 35–36
Finley, Ashley, 36
Fullinwider, Robert K., 24, 55

G

Godinez Ballón, Estella, 39
graduate and professional schools,
    26–27, 45, 63
Granfield, Robert, 45
guidance counselors, 20–21

H

habitus, 14
Hamilton, Laura T., 46, 57
Hart, Jeni, 34, 46
Haveman, Robert, 22
hidden curriculum, 32–34, 38–39
high school experience. *see* precollege
    experience, effect of
Horvat, Erin McNamara, 16

Hubbard, Jennifer, 34, 46
Hurst, Allison L., 25, 29, 45, 65

I

imposter syndrome, 44–45
Indiana Twenty-First Century Scholars, 57

J

Jensen, Barbara, 1, 3, 41
Johnson, David W., 40
Johnson, Roger T., 40
Jones, Stephanie, 37

K

King, Jacqueline E., 56

L

Lareau, Annette, 16, 17
legacy admissions. *see* college choice and college
    admission
  study of, 37–38
Lehmann, Wolfgang, 14, 50
Lichtenberg, Judith, 24, 55
Lindquist, Julie, 31
living-learning programs, 49
low-income first-generation and working-class
    students (LIFGWC), 50–51
Lu, Elissa C., 25
Lubrano, Alfred, 46
Lundy-Wagner, Valerie, 56

M

Martinez, Julia A., 62
mathematics and precollege experience, 20
Matthys, Mick, 31, 49
McLoughlin, Paul J., 48
McNair, Tia, 36
McNamee, Stephen J., 16
meritocracy, myth of, 7, 19, 32, 37
middle class
  advantage of, 12
  child rearing model, 23

habitus of, 14
Miller, Robert K. Jr., 16
Morales, Erik E., 39
Mortenson, Thomas G., 26

N

networks, social. *see* social capital

O

Oldfield, Kenneth, 1, 67
O'Neil, Tara, 24

P

parents of working-class students, 3
Passeron, Jean-Claude, 14
peer leaders and mentors, 47, 49–50, 53, 58, 59
Pell Grants. see finance and financial aid issues
Perna, Laura W., 56
pivotal moment framework, 53–54
poststructuralism, 11
precollege experience, 20
   bridge programs, 61–62
   college and precollege partnerships, 58–59
   College Possible and guidance, 55
   dropout rates, 22
   effect of, 19–21
   high school mentor, effect on college, 58
   parental involvement and support, 59–61
   University of Nebraska college preparatory
      courses, 59
Putnam, Robert D., 17

Q

Quinn, Jocey, 14

R

Rice, Condoleeza, 67
Ronald E. McNair Program, 63
Rose, Stephen, 22
Rubenstein, Ross, 25
Ryan, Jake, 2, 44

S

Sackrey, Charles, 2, 44
SAT cultural bias, 21
Schwartz, Jana L., 44, 46
Seider, Maynard, 44
Simmons, Leigh Ann, 60
Smith, Karl A., 40
social capital
   acquisition of, 17
   definition, 17
   social networks and, 17, 46, 47, 50, 53
social class. *see also* middle class; upper class;
      working-class students
   economic and cultural differences, 45
   impact of, 12, 68
   social identity groups, 4–6, 50
   stereotypes, 6–7
   and upward mobility, 7–8
   visibility, 2, 13, 30, 36–37, 39, 45, 51, 64–66
social reproduction, theory of, 11–12
   social class culture of, 12
social space, 12
Socioeconomic Acceptance and Diversity
      Alliance, 50
Soria, Krista M., 3, 25, 36, 49, 57
Soto, Rhonda, 4
Starr, Brian, 24
Stebleton, Michael J., 49
Stephens, Nicole M., 33, 38
Stevens, Mitchell L., 23
St. John, Edward P., 56–57
Stuber, Jenny M., 43, 44, 65
student employment, 46–47
"symbolic violence." *see* cultural capital

T

Tadal, Teran, 56
Terenzini, Patrick T., 34
Tinto, Vincent, 49
transfer students, missed opportunities, 36
TRIO programs, 59, 63

U

U/Fused, 50
United for Undergraduate Socioeconomic
    Diversity, 50
University of Minnesota free iPads, 57
University of Nebraska college preparatory
    courses, 59
University of Wisconsin textbook rental, 57
upper class, 12
    cultural capital and, 15–17
Upward Bound, 59
Ursinus College free laptops, 57

V

Vagle, Mark D., 37
Vander Putten, Jim, 67

W

Wacquant, Loïc J.D., 16, 17
Walpole, Marybeth, 47
Warnock, Deborah, 50–51
Washington State Achievers, 57
Weiner, Brad, 25, 57
Wilson, Kathryn, 22
working-class students. *see also* finance and
    financial aid issues
    alienation of, 12, 45, 48
    anti-intellectualism of, 30–31
    college choice process of, 23–24
    comfort level in higher education
        institutions, 13–14, 43
    conflicting expectations, 5–6
    definition of, 2
    degree attainment rates and outcomes,
        25–27
    dropping out and habitus, 14–15
    faculty and peer generalizations about,
        30–31
    loyalists, renegades and double agents, 15
    precollege experience, 19–21

relations with faculty, 29, 32
relations with peers, 29, 45, 46, 48–50
social integration, 47, 51
upward social mobility, impact on, 44
work ethic of, 62–63
working-class students, impediments to success,
    34–36
cultural barriers, 1
invisibility of, 9, 30, 36, 39, 51

Y

Yee, April, 56

Z

Zandy, Janet, 39

About the Author

Krista M. Soria works as an analyst with the Office of Institutional Research at the University of Minnesota, Twin Cities. Her research interests include the experiences of first-generation and working-class students in higher education; high-impact practices that promote undergraduates' development and success; and programmatic efforts to enhance college students' leadership development, civic responsibility, and engagement in social change. Soria has worked for more than a decade in higher education, serving as an admissions advisor, TRIO education advisor, and academic advisor. She is presently serving as an adjunct faculty member at the University of Minnesota, Hamline University, St. Mary's University of Minnesota, and St. Cloud State University. Soria holds a doctorate in educational policy and administration (higher education emphasis) from the University of Minnesota, Twin Cities.